Testimonials

RTIR Blurb

Whenever a new baby is born, someone usually says, "Good luck with your kid, because he doesn't come with an instruction manual!" Well, Kerri Yarsley, a successful mother of four, is about to change all that. *The Instruction Manual for Kids – Parent's Edition* is an eminently readable, informative and entertaining book that takes the reader on a journey from pre-pregnancy preparation all the way through to the late teenage years. It covers the basics as well as some interesting behavioural perspectives that you might not expect in a parenting book. So whether you have one or many kids, be prepared to change your thoughts, words, and actions, and have a brilliant and joyful life with your amazing kids.

Bill Statham, author of "The Chemical Maze Shopping Companion"

This comprehensive book sets out many "rules of engagement" between children and their environment during the formative years from birth to early adulthood. Written specifically for parents – both new and seasoned – the book contains information that makes practical sense on all levels. If you are a resident of Planet Earth, then I highly recommend Kerri's book to you. It will inform, amuse, inspire and move you.

Ric Bratton, broadcaster of "This Week In America"

It is my pleasure to share Kerri Yarsley's "The Instructional Manual for Kids – Parent's Edition" with our national radio audience. Having four children all within a six year span, Kerri is superbly qualified to do a book about parenting. She covers every aspect from birth to the teen years thoroughly and candidly in this highly readable, honest, charming, humorous and knowledgeable book. "The Instruction Manual for Kids" is an excellent read and it will be a valuable resource for future reference. Chapters reflect various stages of a child's development and common problems. Kerri's insight helped me understand my fear of water. While reading the book I realized how simple words spoken by my mother instilled a water phobia that still exists. She offers solid advice on how to present the outcome you desire, not the one you fear. In my case the emphasis was on drowning rather than the joys of being in the water. From following your intuition to letting go, "The Instruction Manual for Kids – Parent's Edition" will help you raise independent and capable young adults.

Mila Feldman, mother of two, grandmother of five (including twins)

When my family first met Kerri she had just had her third baby. It was pure joy to observe her kind, confident and relaxed way of communicating and also establishing that loving relationship between the baby and his siblings. I remember thinking I wish my children could acquire some of these skills from Kerri to help them on their journey of raising their own children. Now my wish has been realised with the help of this manual, written by a skillful, generous and understanding human being.

Yvonne, mother of two – aged 5 and 2

I've had quite a few moments with my five year old daughter where I've carried on like a banshee. This is not something I'm proud of at all – quite the opposite in fact. Afterwards, I'd go to bed with the resolve to improve, but that's where it seems to have ended. Now that I've read your strategies it's imprinted the steps in my mind. I feel empowered to follow through and I'm energised to want to. Yes, sometimes the answer is right in front of us, but it takes another person saying it to make us realise it.

Your book has not only made me want to be a better and calmer person, but I now believe that I can be that person.

Rebecca Howl, newly married

Thank you for sharing your experience and wisdom with us all. With great insight to life and living, parenting and partnering, I think Kerri Yarsley has a great perspective on raising children. Although I am not yet a parent, I'm looking forward to referring to this book again in a few years – it's filled with great tips and practical information that Kerri has gained not only through experience, but also from considerable education. I love the mix of light heartedness, scientific and philosophical perspectives. It is a well-balanced and an engaging read for parents-to-be, those already with kids, and even those with children who have flown the coop.

Amy Luttrell

This book is one of the best I've ever read. I would absolutely recommend this to anyone and think it is a must have for any parent! I especially love the part on germs and that we're killing our kids immunities with all these unnecessary 99.9% germ sprays and also the part on keeping babies/kids off sugar for as long as possible. Two things I feel very passionately about!!

The Instruction Manual for Kids

Parent's Edition

Kerri Yarsley

Illustrations by Peter McDonald

BALBOA.
PRESS
A DIVISION OF HAY HOUSE

Book cover design: Shane Cresser
Family Photo (on page 212) © Tim Bamford, Portrait House Photography

Balboa Press books may be ordered through booksellers or by contacting:

Balboa Press
A Division of Hay House
1663 Liberty Drive
Bloomington, IN 47403
www.balboapress.com
1 (877) 407-4847

Printed in the United States of America.

ISBN: 978-1-4525-2325-5 (sc)
ISBN: 978-1-4525-2327-9 (hc)
ISBN: 978-1-4525-2326-2 (e)

Library of Congress Control Number: 2014918083

Balboa Press rev. date: 10/20/2014

This book is dedicated to all parents and their kids.
May you understand and love each other completely and unconditionally.

Contents

Preface

This little book was unconsciously devised over a long period of time, mainly during the teenage years of my four children. The concept had been brewing in my subconscious mind until a day or two after I had completed a relatively long contracting stint at one workplace. Over the years, I had spent some interesting times chatting with my colleagues and friends about their family issues and discussing potential remedies for them to try. I suddenly realised I would not be around every day to present an alternate viewpoint. So the decision to write a book, which could be accessed not only by the people I had grown to care about but also by the general population, seemed an obvious conclusion.

The title of the book, likewise, seemed an obvious choice. Whenever a new baby delights the world with their presence, at least one member of their family says, "Good luck, because they don't come with an instruction manual", or words to that effect. Well, here is *The Instruction Manual for Kids* and I hope it will make life just that little bit easier for both parents and kids.

The book is not intended to be the definitive text on solving all problems that may appear during one's parenting timeframe, nor does it intend to over-shadow the advice and opinions that may be provided by child care or health care professionals. Rather, it is a text that has been compiled from many years of personal experience, education, and trial and error. I have not been the *perfect* parent, nor do I claim to be – that is not possible. I have made many mistakes and I continue to do so, but I do believe I have learned much from these and from the mistakes of others, and I have tried to minimise their negative effects. So, please use this book in collaboration with advice you receive from professional resources and remember that each family's circumstances and experiences are unique. With this in mind, I ask you to pardon my unashamed generalisations for the sake of simplicity and clarity.

Whenever you are faced with a decision and have a number of choices, make sure your ultimate choice feels right for you. Decisions that affect yourself and your children require you to thoroughly consider the alternatives that exist and their consequences over time. Use whatever resources you can to help clarify your mind – the internet (at least three different reputable sources), the local library, your trusted friends and relatives, local community support, and your doctor. If you are still confused, then before you go to sleep at night ask yourself, the universe (or whatever your concept of a higher source might be) for help to find a solution to the question and wait for the answer to come to you (hopefully, by morning). Keep asking until you get an answer. Sometimes the answer will come in small individual steps, or it may appear as a complete solution. Listen to your intuitive flashes – they will help direct you.

This manual has been designed to be read initially from start to finish so you, the reader, can get an appreciation of the over-arching strategy to follow and then, as the need arises, you may pick the chapter that best suits your current situation and follow the steps therein.

Some of the small text boxes scattered throughout the book contain personal stories that relate to the preceding content discussion. They are intended to provide an amusing or poignant perspective on the topic. In others, the boxes contain snippets of information that I have found useful to know over the years.

Included in the Bibliography is a list of books and resources I have found extremely useful and interesting, not just in the writing of this book, but as guides for life. I have included the websites that have been referenced throughout the book and also additional websites that may be useful for the parent who wishes to find further information about a specific topic that has been mentioned in the text. My apologies if some of these websites are no longer active.

Please note that the words *children* and *kids* have been used throughout the text for simplicity, however they imply the singular *child* and *kid* and either gender as well. In keeping with the practical English language convention promoting simplicity and clarity, the pronouns *he*, *him*, and *his* are used for nouns incorporating both genders.

The author, her husband, and their four children taken in 1995.

Acknowledgments

Thank you to my children Sean, Amanda, Iain, and Ella, to my parents Ian and Kit Fraser, and to our wonderful pets who all helped to provide much of the material and inspiration for this book.

Thank you to my wonderful reviewers: Rebecca Howl, Dr Renald Portelli, Yvonne, Jay Stephens (from The Herb Cottage), and to each of my kids, for being brave enough to read the manuscript and provide me with excellent feedback and suggestions for improving the content.

Thank you to Bill Statham, the author of *The Chemical Maze* for his wonderfully informative book and support prior to and during the book launch.

Thank you to Peter McDonald for his beautiful illustrations and for patiently interpreting my instructions and multiple adjustments. You have done a truly great job.

A special thank you goes to my husband Frank for not only providing me with feedback on the content and much needed support, encouragement, and guidance during the months of writing, but for the loving years we have shared together in the past and for all of those we will spend together in the future. I could not have done this without you.

1

Introduction

Focus on the outcome you want.

Introduction

This is a book about MIND CONTROL – but wait; before you run away; it might not be the *mind* you are expecting. I'm not talking about you controlling your kids' minds, nor am I talking about your kids controlling your mind. This book is about YOU controlling YOUR mind. This is crucial in your quest to becoming a good parent.

Why? I hear you ask. For the simple reason that for you to be able to guide someone with limited or no life skills, it is better for you to be calm and rational.

How do you start to control your own mind? If you've ever tried it, you know it's not that easy. If you've never tried it, then you may be in for a rude awakening, or at least a bit of a shock. Your mind is apt to run away at the slightest distraction. Try this now. Sit comfortably and observe your mind for 15 seconds – a quarter of a minute. See if you can count how many thoughts you have in this time. Every thought you have must be included – even the ones that say, *This is stupid*, or *I hope nobody's watching me* or *Should I count this thought?* Just observe how many different thoughts come up.

Once you have done this, try it again, only this time focus on one thought. Yes, only one! Pick a thought that will be very interesting to you, so you can pay attention to it. It might be an image of a cherished loved one, your dog or cat, a beautiful tree, a sunset, your favourite car, or motorbike – whatever takes your full attention. Now focus on it completely. Picture it in every minute detail; even down to the tiniest eyelash, leaf, or bolt, with the full intensity and variety of colour. Every time your mind runs away with a distracted thought and you become aware of it, just stop and come back to your first, single thought. Don't beat yourself up mentally if you can't hold the image for long. It can take some time to become adept at it.

If this is your first attempt, you are doing well just giving it a go. The more often you do it, the better you will become and the longer you will be able to hold the image.

These are the first steps to being able to control your own mind, and for you to be the best parent you can be, it is imperative you learn to do this and to do this as well as you are able to do.

The next stage in your progression as a parent is for you to learn how to picture the outcome you want and not the one you most fear. When you were growing up, did you know a person who always seemed calm and relaxed, and made you feel like you wanted to be just like them? I did, and when I imagined myself as that person, I tended to *act* like them and be more in control of myself. You probably did too.

Many of us have been brought up by loving parents with the very best of intentions, but their own experience of a stable or controlled environment is one that has been dominated by fear and retribution: "If you do that, then you'll get a beating!"

In my own experience, an occurrence that typifies this unnecessary struggle for dominance by an older generation over a younger one was one time when my elder brother, elder sister, and I were being scolded by our father for some mischief of which I cannot recall. We were all standing there lined up in front of him – the three of us with solemn faces, heads bowed, and hands clenched behind our backs. As our father stood, towering over us, he asked us with a stern tone, "Do you know what happens when I take off my belt?" My brother and sister looked fearfully at each other, not daring to make a sound, knowing exactly what would happen from their experience of superior years. But then I, the youngest and most innocent, said, "Your pants will fall down?"

What did my father do? Fortunately, he had a great sense of humour so he started laughing and the entire experience became joyful and funny, instead of painful and frightening. This story is remembered for its humour by my family and has been retold many times over the years. Interestingly, the mischief that originally triggered this encounter was not important enough to be remembered. It became lost in the perspective of the moment and was not blown out of proportion just to feed a bruised ego.

I don't criticise my father for his initial response because I know he was doing the best he could at that time given his own training from his parents. That was his only template from which to mould his own parenting model. Back when he was a child, families were just recovering from World War I and then the Great Depression came along. At that time, unemployment levels were around 30% in Australia, and you don't have to be Einstein to recognise that huge stress and strain existed for all families. Many of my father's friends had no shoes to wear to school, and bread and dripping (congealed fat from boiled meats) was a popular meal. Back then, the family structure was strictly adhered to – the *man of the house* was male and he was responsible for providing for the family; the *housewife* was female and she looked after all the domestic duties, including feeding the family on sometimes very meagre earnings; and the kids were *seen and not heard*. Discipline (punishment) in the home was usually preceded by father or mother annoyed by some breach of the family rules. A quick smack on the buttocks or the back of the legs by a firm hand or wooden spoon was the usual treatment, but it was sometimes worse, especially if other stresses existed in the family, such as financial ruin. Corporal punishment was also liberally meted out at school. Any child who showed disrespect – and this was often arbitrarily determined – usually copped a dose of the cuts (leather strap or cane across the hands or backside). Control was a big issue back then and it still is today, but its guise is perhaps a little more subtle, though equally as destructive when out of balance.

And here we come to the crux of the matter – balance. When you, as a person, are in balance, life is brilliant; it flows easily and perfectly. But when you are not in balance, then guess what, the poop hits the fan all the time and starts spraying everything and everyone around you with putrid smelling, sticky stuff. You get angry, sad, emotional, critical, and so on. I'm sure you get the picture.

This is when you need to rely heavily on your belief systems for support and sustenance. This doesn't necessarily mean *religion*. I have often wondered at the justification for some of the worst atrocities around the world and over the ages in the name of religion.

I believe in a system that values ALL life with unconditional love, respect, and trust.

If there is unconditional love, then there is no room for fear or hatred. There are no emotional games to be played, or strings attached to the love that is offered. It is freely given with no expectations.

If there is respect, then there is compassion, consideration, and tolerance. Respect flows all ways – bottom-up, top-down, and side-to-side. Everyone is deserving of respect until they do something to lose it. If it is taken for granted, then it will be lost. It needs constant nurturing. Respect for *all* rules out discrimination in all its guises – racial, gender, intellectual, sexual or vertical! (I am 5'1" and a bit (155cm).)

If there is trust, then there is confidence, honesty, and integrity. When trust exists in a home, then the family members have complete confidence in each other. This provides the basis for balanced self-confidence and healthy self-esteem as the kids grow up. When you are honest in all your dealings, then people can believe what you say. If lying is a part of your MO[1] then you will need to have a very good memory because lies have a way of growing

---

[1]   *modus operandi* (Lat.): method of operating

out of control and you will eventually be discovered for the untruthful things that have been said.

In recent years, the public has become more aware of information relating to the detection of deception or lies, such as the presence of micro facial expressions, inflections of the voice, or a very deep or shallow breath when someone is lying.[2]

When you say what you do and, more importantly, do what you say, then people know exactly where they stand with you. Whether your actions are good or bad, people know what to expect from you if you have this type of integrity. Your word is your bond and you are considered reliable in all you do or say. This is very comforting for the people around you because there is a high degree of predictability about you. Your reputation is at stake if you don't deliver what you say you will. When you keep your reputation and integrity intact, then you are deemed to be trustworthy. This is worth something in life and it's worth preserving.

All life is deserving of love, respect, and trust. So, next time you see a spider in your shower, collect him gently and free him outside. He is only there to catch some insects for his food. Not only does he have the right to live out his life as much as you do, but you will feel *good* about releasing him, and provide positive values for your children to emulate. Obviously, if you suffer from arachnophobia[3] then you may be hard pressed to look at it, let alone pick it up, so do what you can do and do it with compassion, not fear.

We had a snake – fortunately only a carpet python – wrapped around the handle of our BBQ. It had been lying there probably attempting to hibernate over the cooler winter months.

While considering our options, I grabbed it securely around the neck, close to its head, so it couldn't turn around and bite me. Then I grabbed it somewhere between its middle and its tail. It started to coil quite strongly around my arm and when I placed it over my shoulders I decided that this probably wasn't such a good idea because my neck may have been exposed to its coils – not good to be strangled by a snake that I was trying to help! It was only about one metre long and about 2-3cm in diameter, so not too daunting.

---

[2]   Ekman, P. *Telling Lies*, 2009; pg 43
[3]   An unusually strong fear of spiders.

> After showing the kids and my husband taking a photo or two, I released it on the other side of our property. At no time did I feel fear or anxiety for my safety and after the initial snatch, the snake also calmed down. When I released it, it didn't turn on me and attempt to bite me, it simply slithered off among the long grass. I believe that it learned we meant it no harm, so it relaxed and went on with life. I guess if it had been one of the venomous varieties, like a Brown Snake, we would have chosen a different path and had a snake-catcher come and take it away. But, it wasn't a *baddie* and I was very grateful.

I mention this story not to illustrate how heroic I was (some might say stupid), but to show you the Law of Attraction[4] in action. The snake was a relatively harmless one, so we, as a family, were not attracting harm to our environment. I was not fearful, so the snake recognised there was no need to fear. We both survived the encounter intact and feeling good about it – at least I was, and I assume the snake was OK, if not a little perturbed at being displaced.

So, be careful about what you think because this will attract more of it – good or bad – into your life. If you have a value system that is based on love, respect, and trust in place in your home, you can create a small world of happiness and joy for all your family because that is what you will attract into your lives. Remember to picture the *best* outcome.

Also, have *fun* in what you do, especially with your kids! You don't have to spend lots of money creating a fun time either. What's the point of spending up big on toys or an expensive holiday if you're not there (in mind) to share it with them. You might be sitting next to your kids while they play with their new toys, but if you're worrying about how you're going to pay off the credit card bills, or you're spending all your time answering mobile phone calls from work or messaging friends on social media, then the quality of your time spent with your kids is completely lost. When you spend time with your kids, be there completely – body, heart, and mind. This will ensure your kids get the most out of the occasion and so will you. This type of focussed activity will give you the necessary time to recover from the rigours of a busy life, where you are trying to juggle work, home, and your own personal commitments.

---

[4]   Like attracts like – you attract into your life what is predominately in your thoughts and feelings.

> I remember as a young kid having a fantastic time at the beach during the summer holidays. I used to roam around the sand dunes and creep through the tea-tree pretending I was a spy or one of Robin Hood's merry men (there was no political correctness back then!).
>
> But the greatest time was when my dad used to dive into the water and swim and play with us kids, in spite of the dog paddling along after him and clawing him (or any of us, actually) when he caught up.
>
> These were happy and simple times and the best part was sharing the occasion and being in the present. We felt so special and loved. These times made up for the ones when dad was working late or involved with committees.

If you are stuck at any time and are unsure what to do, remember what it was like when you were a kid. Put yourself in your kids' shoes and view the day from their perspective with all their innocence and hope. Remember the excitement you had when exploring new things and places. Remember the feeling of joy and satisfaction when you accomplished something; no matter how small or insignificant it might seem now. In general, kids see the world in black and white. As adults, we recognise that there are many grey areas, so forgive your kids for their inexperience and don't humiliate, ridicule or judge them for it.

If you feel anger rising, close your eyes, breathe in deeply and smoothly, breathe out twice as slowly, and *smile*. This will quieten your mood and release some tension and frustration.

Words said in anger and actions performed in anger are highly destructive at a physical level and also at the emotional and mental levels. Not only do they affect the recipient (who you're targeting), but yourself as well!

If you could step out of your skin and observe what is happening to you at this very point in time, you would probably notice how red-faced you are, your eyes might be wide and black, you might even be shaking or trembling slightly, your blood pressure is up, and you look like something out of a horror movie. Imagine what fear this is creating in your child, and imprinting in his sponge-like mind. You are becoming a monster to him, and creating an environment for him to be scared of you, as well as creating a few more grey hairs for yourself. This is not the type of behaviour that will encourage your child to open up to you as he grows older. Do you think he will want to share his inner-most secrets and dreams with you? Not likely! He would rather store them up in his memory and contemplate them in silence, or with his trusted friends, than risk sharing with an abusive parent. This loss to you is huge! It may be years before you realise it, but nothing is worth this type of loss and as a parent, you need to remember this point.

So, avoid using angry words and actions, especially as a common form of discipline or control. A situation should never get that far. This is where a system of boundaries will set the limits and enable you to keep your balance during the times of trouble and doubt. Reflect upon your past actions at the end of the day and really think about how things could have been handled better and practice it in your mind for next time.

To summarise, you need to be able to control your mind and your thoughts. If you let them run away, then anything could happen. Keep fear under control and in perspective. Picture the most desirable result for every situation that presents itself to you and stick with it. And have fun while you're kids are at home with you. The growth cycle of your child is relatively fast and so incredibly fascinating that if you open your mind to it, you will learn so much, and realise that you can share in a great deal of joy in the process.

This is your kid we're talking about, so don't do anything less than the best you can for him, for yourself, and for a happy life together.

2

Preparation or Get a Pet

A young pet in the house is a bit like having a baby.

Instructions:

1. Read the Introduction.
2. Buy a young pet of the type and breed you like best.
3. Create a safe and secure environment.
4. Be fair and consistent with your behaviour.
5. Keep well-defined boundaries.
6. Be as physically fit as you can be.
7. Let love and compassion motivate you.
8. Make the decision to have a baby.
9. Share your new baby experience with your pet.

So, you're thinking seriously about having a kid. Then you need to prepare not only your mind, but also your body.

Buy a young pet of the type and breed you like best

One of the best things you can do is to get yourself a pet – preferably a domesticated one! If you have been blessed with growing up with a family pet, then choose the one with which you already have an affinity. In other words, make it easier on yourself and go with what you know. If you consider yourself a *cat* person, then buy a kitten. If you have grown up with or love dogs, then buy a puppy. If you're not sure, go to a reputable pet supplier and ask their advice. Just remember it is well known that dogs have masters, but cats have slaves! Many of my cat-loving friends totally agree with me on this, and are still perfectly content to show loyal devotion to their feline masters. It's worth it.

If you're not ready to commit to a *large* pet just yet, then you might like to try a guinea pig or other small rodent. Sometimes people like to have birds, reptiles, fish or other non-mammals as pets. These are fine as pets, but might not be as challenging to keep as a young mammal, which is closer to a human baby and usually needs more care.

Once you have decided on a pet, you need to commit to it and buy a young one. For simplicity, I shall illustrate this chapter using a dog as my preferred choice for a pet. Please substitute your choice of pet. The type of pet and detail for each will vary, but the process is generally the same.

You and your partner now need to go out and choose a puppy. For the sake of your sanity, decide on a breed that will best suit yourselves and your circumstances. If you live in an apartment, you need to check if you are allowed to have a dog on the premises. Sometimes small lap dogs, such as the Chihuahua or King Charles Cavalier breeds are acceptable in these circumstances, as they are easily controllable and don't require much space for comfortable living. If you live in a detached house and have some yard space, you should be able to have whichever breed you like as long as you cater for their individual needs. If you live on acreage, then you can choose a breed that loves to run all day, such as a Kelpie or Australian Cattledog.

As a rule of thumb, your dog will be happier, less destructive, and more obedient if you exercise it regularly – preferably daily. We used to have Cattledogs in the suburbs before we had any children and they helped us keep fit. We took them for an eight km run every other morning before work. They just loved it and were always ready to go. Now, please don't think you have to get out there and beat the pavement every spare moment of the day. What I suggest you find is a balance that works for you. A simple 30 minute walk once a day will be beneficial to your new pup and to yourself.

You don't need to worry about a pure breed either; mutts are just as lovable and loyal. In my experience, the cross breeds are often healthier animals because they have a wider and more varied gene pool, so they may not be as prone to debilitating genetic disorders as some pure breeds. This can save you heart-ache as well as money in vet fees and specialised food or medicines.

Ensure the breeder or pet supplier gives you comprehensive information about the care and handling of your new pet. This is especially important if you have not cared for a pet before. Listen well and make no assumptions about your current knowledge.

Create a safe and secure environment

When you arrive home, introduce your new family member to his new environment. Make sure it is safe and secure for him so he feels comfortable. A small room, such as the laundry, is a good starting place because you can usually close it off and keeping it clean is comparatively easy. Puppies have many needs and these include:

- Multiple feeding each day
- Fresh water available anytime
- Clean bedding

- Newspaper for toilet training
- Gentle handling
- Toys for playing and chewing
- Lots of attention, patience, and love

The first couple of weeks are usually the hardest as you become used to a new living, breathing, demanding, and noisy creature in your house. He will take up what seems like a huge amount of time and energy, and you may feel exhausted at the end of each day. Then you discover the night feeds and realise the day hasn't finished. Or has it just started? Depending on the age of your pet, these days may just wash into each other with no defined structure, and you might start to feel like a wrung out dishcloth. But, believe me, it's all worth it. Keep on doing what needs to be done, and this period will be over in a few short weeks.

Be fair and consistent with your behaviour

The most important thing for you to keep in mind is to be consistent. Set aside a specific place for your pet to sleep, eat, and toilet, and keep taking him back to those places for that specific purpose. Introduce him to the outside with care, making sure he cannot escape under fences or gates. Yes, he is little and cute and so adorable you want to play all day with him and take a million pictures of him, but he needs to know you are the boss too. Be prepared to say *No* to him in a deep voice to show you mean it. Physically stop him from going into areas he is not allowed to go and repeat *No* as often as necessary. He is young and ignorant of the *Big Bad World*, so you need to teach him the difference. Allowing him to run around freely and to go wherever he likes is potentially dangerous or destructive, especially if you live near a busy road, or are the proud owner of a beautiful garden or vegetable patch. It also teaches him that there are no rules and this is to be avoided at all costs.

Keep well-defined boundaries

This is the time when TRAINING starts and I'm not only talking about your pet's training, but yours as well. Here is where you start to build good boundaries. Pets can be spoilt as easily as children, but the impact can be identified in a few weeks compared with years for humans. Puppy schools are an excellent choice of training facility and many veterinary clinics offer this service. The basic rules of training and obedience are taught and applied in an environment that is safe and encouraging for both students – animal and human. Your puppy should be taught to socialise with other animals and kids before 13 weeks old.

Be as physically fit as you can be

The next important thing you need to do to prepare yourself for parenthood is to be as physically fit as you could possibly be given your current lifestyle. This will help you in a number of ways, not the least in mum's recovery after the labour and delivery, but also for your quality of life in general. If you do nothing more than take a walk for 30 minutes a day, or every other day, then that's a great start. And if you have an energetic puppy to enjoy it with, that's a fantastic way to start any day. The bonds of friendship and loyalty you build with your pet from the start of your relationship together are immeasurable and last a lifetime.

My husband and I were fitness freaks and the first few years of our marriage were spent doing activities like judo, running, swimming, kayaking, and rock climbing.

My husband used to run many fun runs and a few marathons and he often took our older cattledog on many of these. She loved to be by his side and even made it into the papers one time. On another occasion, she was running freely with him over a marathon distance (42km, 26mi), but because she kept running off to the side and sniffing all sorts of things (as dogs tend to do) my husband and the runners near-by estimated she must have covered twice the distance, and yet, after they crossed the finish line, she looked as keen to go as when she started!

We qualified as Fitness Leaders (aka gym instructors) the year before my first child was born. This gave us the knowledge we needed to not only train ourselves, but other like-minded people as well. That same year, I decided to train for and run a marathon – only it was more like jogged, walked, and hobbled! It took me over five hours to finish and one of my first thoughts after finishing was, "Having a baby MUST be easier than this!" Well, less than a year later, I found out.

I firmly believe that my relatively high level of fitness prior to and during each of my four pregnancies helped me to have an uncomplicated gestation period, a quick labour experience using little or no drugs, and an excellent post-natal recovery. So, get out there with your puppy, enjoy the morning (and/or afternoon) walk, smell a few roses along the way, and get fit.

Let love and compassion motivate you

You love your pet and you want him to live a happy life. This means you need to be happy too. If you follow the basic and simple rules from the start, you will enjoy the fruits of a loving and obedient buddy. The time with your pet should be fun and joyous, so make it so.

Now that you have tested the water with your pet and no doubt made a few mistakes along the way – don't worry, we all do – you should start to feel that rearing a child is possible. The timeframe lasts a bit longer though, so where a pet develops over weeks and months, a child will develop over months and years (decades). Be aware that many people choose to stop at this point. Their pet becomes their *child* and they put their energies into nurturing and fostering this image of their offspring.

Make the decision to have a baby

Now that you've decided to have a baby, there is no turning back. Most pregnancies differ, so I will share my experiences with you. Be aware that you may feel the same things; or you may feel less or more of the same things; or you may feel completely different things. Remember that your mind plays a big part of your experience here too. So focus on the best possible outcome for your circumstances.

The first sign of my pregnancy was tender nipples. Then I began to feel like I had mild indigestion, which plain salted cracker biscuits eaten before getting out of bed helped to alleviate. Fortunately, I didn't have any morning sickness and I could eat most of the things I normally ate as a vegetarian. Also, my sense of smell was heightened quite dramatically – almost to superpower status. Back in those days, smoking was allowed in the office space, so I had a negative ion generator (NIG) on my desk. Every time a smoker went past, I stuck my nose right next to the NIG so I wouldn't inhale any of the toxins from the smoke. I would also give the offender a piece of my mind. Actually, I was a bit of a mini-tyrant when it came down to it.

> My husband used to boil lamb shanks for the dogs as a treat. I remember coming home from work one day – after driving through the peak hour traffic for the previous 40 minutes and feeling more than a little hot and bothered – and I was looking forward to relaxing and putting my feet up. As I walked in the front door, the disgusting smell of fatty, boiling meat made me retch and practically bowled me over. I was ready to head straight back to work because the painful drive home was nothing compared with the nauseating affront to my pregnancy-induced super senses. Boy, did he cop it!

As my pregnancy progressed, we continued our fitness regime, though I reduced the strength exercises (weights) and maintained the cardiac exercises (aerobics). This kept blood pressure under control and endurance levels high – very important for the labour process and the first three months or so after delivery. My first labour lasted six hours – a bit over my marathon time – and it wasn't easier, mainly because of the unknown element and the increased *scare* factor. The midwife kept telling me I was doing really well and my requests for pain relief were answered eventually with pethidene and gas – which, in hindsight, I felt did nothing to ease the pain, but merely made me fall asleep between contractions. I felt like I had lost what little control I had of the labour process. In the end, I needed assistance using a Ventouse extractor (suction-cup device) to help pull out the baby by his head. But, as soon as my baby was born, the pain just stopped like a switch being flicked off. I felt terrific, despite the fact that my face was covered in spots because I had burst blood vessels all over the place pushing so hard during the final stage of labour. And then suddenly, right there in front of me in my arms, was this little being – dark pink and wrinkly, with a screwed up face and bald head, covered in white slime (vernix[5]), and so totally perfect. He was so small and utterly dependant, my heart just opened completely to him. It was a defining moment in my life.

---

[5]   Vernix caseosa: the oily mixture covering the foetus during the last three months in the womb.

My second labour only lasted three hours and my gorgeous daughter was born; she was equally perfect and miraculous. My third labour was around 90 minutes – after which my son's head was in such perfect shape that he looked like he had had a Caesarean birth – and my last labour, after waiting about 5½ hours for any contractions to commence after my waters broke, took about 45 minutes. I can remember the nurse's amazement as I lightly pushed my wheelchair following my postpartum shower. I felt fantastic! For each of these latter three deliveries, I had no drugs; I maintained good breath control and relaxed between each severe contraction – I used to repeat the word *RELAX* before and during contractions, a bit like a mantra. It made a big difference to my physical as well as mental state. And short labours are definitely the way to go! So, girls, if you do nothing else, focus on and embrace the feelings of a quick labour *before* you go into labour. You might just make your experience of the labour process less painful and drawn out.

Share your new baby experience with your pet

The introduction between your new baby and your pet should be a warm and loving experience for everyone, including your pet!

When we came home from the hospital with our brand new bundle of joy, we sat on the floor with the new baby wrapped in a bunny rug and encouraged the dogs to sniff and explore this new creature. We were right there and carefully watched the whole event unfold – all the while reassuring the dogs with welcoming words, pats on the head and other comforting gestures.

Because we were relaxed, calm, and confident, the dogs did not feel anything strange or out of place. The baby showed complete trust and innocence, and the dogs recognised that there was no threat. They accepted each of our new babies in turn when they arrived home and were loving, loyal, and protective companions to all of them.

Have a child if it is physically possible for you to do so. If you let him, he will teach you as much about life as you can teach him.

3

Anatomy of a Kid

Looks can be deceiving.

Instructions:

1. Read the Introduction.
2. Understand some of the body's systems.
3. Provide good nutritious foods.
4. Give your kids water to drink.
5. Exercise your kids to get oxygen flowing.
6. Avoid eating too many sweet or fatty foods.
7. Get rid of the toxins and wastes.
8. Did I mention to give your kids water to drink?
9. Purchase food for the right reason.
10. See your General Practitioner (GP) if you're unsure.

This chapter may be a little tough going for some, but persist with it and see if you can understand what amazing bodies we have.

Kids may look familiar, but they have differences no doctor or scanner can see. For example, they have at least two stomachs: one for normal food, and the other for dessert. No matter how much they may whinge and complain that they can't eat another thing from the plate in front of them, they will *always* have room for dessert!

Anăt´omў   **n. Dissection; science of bodily structure; anatomical structure; analysis[6]**

The above definition implies a very clinical and scientific analysis, but rather than limit the dissection and analysis to a structural one, I would like to focus on this topic from a parent's perspective.

Understand some of the body's systems

The human body is a fascinating thing. It is made up of so many things from the tiniest cells up to the most intricate systems and organs that we can see and touch. Our brain controls this myriad of systems and regulates our body's normal functioning.

---

[6]   *The Concise Oxford Dictionary (5th Edition)*, 1964; pg 42.

The body's main systems include:

Nervous System	This is the controlling system of our bodies. Messages pass to and from the brain via nerves or chemicals in the blood. Some parts of this system are under voluntary control where we can consciously make something happen, like talking. But, the vast majority of this system is under involuntary (autonomic) control where it automatically takes care of our bodies, generally without our knowledge.
Circulatory System	One of the internal transportation systems composed of the blood, arteries, veins, capillaries and heart. This is a bit like a major infrastructure system because it is a two-way system that transports nutrients and oxygen throughout the body and also takes away some waste products, like carbon dioxide.
Digestive System	This is the system that helps provide our body with the nutrition it needs by converting the food we eat into a simple form that can be absorbed into the blood stream and used by the body's cells. Any undigested food, cellular waste, mucus, and bowel micro-organisms are excreted as faeces via the lower Digestive System (Alimentary System).
Endocrine System	This system is made up of a number of glands throughout the body which produce chemicals called hormones. Along with the Autonomic Nervous System, these can affect the internal functions within the body by stimulating the activity of specific organs – a bit like a coach motivating the team to peak performance.
Lymphatic System	This is the basis of our immune system. It is another internal transportation system comprising lymph vessels and lymph nodes. This system is closely aligned with the Circulatory System and it's like a rubbish disposal system because it's one-way and it removes larger waste matter, such as damaged cells and micro-organisms.

Respiratory System	With each in-breath, this system passes oxygen from the lungs into the blood stream for our cells to use. Carbon dioxide is then removed as waste with each exhalation.
Reproductive System	This is the system that enables us to have kids. It is different for males and females because each has a very specific task to do. Males produce a cell called a sperm cell and females produce an ovum or egg cell. When these two combine, the now fertilised cell has the potential to grow into a human baby.
Skeletal System	This is our bony foundation and structural support system. Without it, we would be a gooey mess on the ground.
Muscular System	This system enables us to move. It works mainly with the Skeletal System and is attached to the bones by tendons at defined points to help bend joints and cause our bones to move in specific ways.
Urinary System	This is a filtering system that passes out liquid waste products via the familiar yellow-coloured fluid called urine.

The cells of the body have some simple needs to survive: food, water, oxygen, and the removal of wastes. If their environment maintains this basic structure, then they will happily live to their fullest and healthiest extent. As an added benefit, good nutrition feeds not only the body, but also the mind and the behaviour.

Provide good nutritious foods

At the physical level, our body is composed of approximately 60-70% water[7] and the remaining 30-40% is typically composed of 11-15% protein, 12-18% fat, and 7% minerals.[8] These percentages have varied since the

---

[7]   Ross, J.S. & Wilson, K.J.W. *Foundations of Anatomy and Physiology* 5th Edition, 1981; pg 53.

[8]   www.answers.com/topic/composition-of-the-body

1970's mainly due to the tendency to choose highly fatty fast food, rather than prepare our own meals.[9] Variations also exist between individuals and genders, as males tend to have a higher proportion of protein than women because they generally have a larger muscle mass. Women tend to have a higher proportion of body fat than males. This is necessary for the normal functioning of a woman's body, such as menstruation and breast feeding.

With these proportions in mind, it makes sense to either eat foods with similar proportions as a whole food, or to eat a variety of foods that will make up the proportions as a group. The latter is easier to achieve and more satisfying in general because we like to try different things with many flavours and textures. This helps our palate develop so we can appreciate foods from all over the world.

You can formulate a diet for yourself and your family to suit your particular preferences as long as it provides the essential nutrients needed by the human body. The table below[10] provides you with these essential nutrients and a sample of the mostly natural and unprocessed food sources that can be used to obtain them.

Nutrient	Function	Sources[11]
Protein	To provide amino acids for the proper maintenance of the body's cells; for enzyme and hormone production; and for blood protein production. An excess of protein causes the nitrogenous part to be converted to fat and stored in the body's fat deposits.	Soya beans, lentils, eggs, meat, broccoli, fish, peas, garlic, mushrooms, sundried tomatoes.

9   In 1970 in the USA, $6 billion was spent on fast food. In 2001, that figure had escalated to $110 billion. Sourced from *Fast Food Nation* (2002) by Eric Schlosser; pg 3.

10   Based on information from Ross, J.S. & Wilson, K.J.W. *Foundations of Anatomy and Physiology* 5th Edition, 1981; pg 108-12.

11   *NUTTAB 2006 (Australian Food Composition Tables)*, Food Standards Australia New Zealand, 2006

Nutrient	Function	Sources[11]
Fats	To produce energy and heat; to provide fatty acids to support certain organs, such as, the eyes or kidneys; to transport fat-soluble vitamins; to form cholesterol; are present within the nerve sheaths; and within sebaceous secretions of the skin. An excess of fat is stored in the fat deposits.	Dairy foods, meat, fish, oils from animal or plant sources, nuts.
Carbohydrate	To provide energy and heat. Complex carbohydrates, such as pasta and rice, take longer to digest and are stored in the muscles and ready to use as an energy source after about 36 hours. Simple carbohydrates, like sugar, are readily digested and absorbed into the blood stream within minutes. An excess of carbohydrate is converted to fat and stored in the body's fat deposits, such as under the skin.	Sugar, pasta, rice, cereals, bread, biscuits, sweets, dried fruits, potatoes.
Vitamins	To ensure that certain essential bodily functions occur for good health. There are two main groups: Fat-soluble vitamins – A, D, E & K Water-soluble vitamins – B complex & C	Green leafy vegetables, carrots, eggs, dairy, cereals, nuts, fruits, legumes, meat.
Mineral Salts	To ensure all bodily processes occur. These are inorganic compounds and are usually required in the body in small or trace quantities – Calcium, Phosphorus, Sodium, Iron, Iodine, Potassium, Magnesium, Manganese, and Selenium.	Green leafy vegetables, dairy, eggs, meat, oatmeal, wholemeal bread.
Water	To hydrate the body for essential functions.	Water, fruits, vegetables, eggs, dairy.

Nutrient	Function	Sources[11]
Fibre	To provide bulk to the food we eat so we are no longer hungry and to ensure that the bowel functions normally to eliminate waste from the body by stimulating effective peristalsis.[12]	Garlic, chilli, lentils, legumes, rice bran, firm tofu, sundried tomatoes, popcorn, falafels.

A simple diet to follow is one that provides complex carbohydrates as an energy source; protein for muscle development, and cellular and enzymatic functions; essential fats, vitamins, and minerals for well run bodily processes; enough fibre to be able to get rid of most wastes; and plenty of water to lubricate the whole thing

> Before kids, my husband and I followed a regular exercise routine each day – jogging alternated with swimming or kayaking. We used to eat a fairly large breakfast comprising anything from pasta, porridge, scrambled eggs, wholemeal toast, freshly squeezed orange juice, fresh fruit, yoghurt, and muesli. Lunch was sandwiches, or leftovers from the previous evening's meal, and dinner was anything from hearty soups, pasta dishes or casseroles with rice in winter, to Asian-inspired stir fries and salads in summer. We tended to follow the *Kingly breakfast*, *Queenly lunch*, and *Princely dinner* routine, which worked in well with doing gym sessions or martial arts in the evenings because you didn't feel like having a big meal after strenuous exercise.
>
> After the kids arrived, time moved differently and the days seemed to be spent eating a meal, cleaning up after the meal, or preparing for the next one. The kids' meals were generally always freshly made and initially started with fairly bland food – mashed bananas, stewed apples (without added sugar) and scrambled eggs. Later on we gradually introduced tastier and bulkier foods as their digestive systems developed.

When the body receives the correct proportion of nutrients, it will function correctly. It's not rocket science, it's simple – stay in balance.

---

[12] The rhythmic contraction and release of muscles encircling the walls of the alimentary tract.

Give your kids water to drink

Keep in mind that water is the main ingredient in our bodies, because it does so much for us. It keeps the hidden cells of our bodies moist; is a major component of blood and tissue fluid; it assists with the regulation of our body's temperature through perspiration – our own unique air conditioning system; and participates in all our chemical reactions; just to name a few. So it should be the highest on our list of consumables. That's pretty easy to do if you always carry a water bottle with you and sip from it every half hour or so.

Drinking an unchilled glass of filtered or purified water before each meal will hydrate you and because it is at room temperature it should pass through your stomach quickly, rather than cause a contraction due to the cold. So when you eat the food, your digestion will not be prolonged due to the dilution of the acid in your stomach. Some people also feel a sense of satiety earlier so they don't feel like eating as much.

Give your kids water to drink everyday and all through the day. Everything else is second rate. You may also notice that thirsty kids can often misbehave, so supply lots of water in small quantities. Your kids copy your actions, so let them see you drink water throughout the day and they will be happier to do it too. We all need it!

Exercise your kids to get oxygen flowing

When you have the nutritional aspects under control, the next thing to do is to ensure the flow of oxygen is passing unrestricted through your kid's body. This means lots of big deep breaths and muscle movement. Combine the two and you have – EXERCISE!!

Kids love exercise because it's not a chore to them – it's fun! This can be one of the easiest or hardest things to do with your kids. It's up to you. Exercising with your kids is a great way to bond with them and they will watch you closely and learn from your behaviour. The foundations you set in place here will lead to the sharing of many more times and different tasks as your kids grow.

The best way to go about it is to work out a list of fun activities to do, create a very flexible schedule, and ask for your child's input. Kids have some great ideas and you might learn something from them. Also, you may need to let them down gently if a trip to the moon isn't a possibility today. Mind you, kids have a brilliant imagination, and you might be amazed what a cardboard box can become – especially a big one discarded from a new appliance or entertainment system. The surface of the moon is not necessarily that far away – just throw in a few cushions, an old doona, and poke out some stars, planets, and comets on the box sides, and *voila*, you have a moon! Keep the lid flaps on to close up the box and it becomes all dark in there – just like the real thing! Your kid can jump around inside the box in relative safety; burning up energy, and staying healthy and happy.

The important thing here is movement. This is good for two reasons:

1. Life-sustaining oxygen is circulating within your kid's body; and
2. He will need a nap after this, so you can *both* have a rest.

Avoid eating too many sweet or fatty foods

How many times do people get sick or just feel poorly after they have had a celebratory dinner, such as Christmas? We all tend to over indulge on these occasions because they're only once a year, so we eat like we haven't seen food for a week. Then, after a day or so, when we've recovered from painfully bloated stomachs, we might notice that we've picked up a cold or worse. Why does it happen?

One reason this might occur is due to the imbalance of chemicals flowing through our bodies. When your bodily fluids are in their normal state you feel good and perform better. These fluids include the blood, the fluid within your cells (intracellular fluid), and the fluid surrounding your internal organs (intercellular fluid). The blood is the major transport system within the body for food, oxygen, and infections, and when it is in a more acidic state, some infections will flourish because they prefer a slightly acidic environment. That's why we can feel really bad after eating a lot of sweet or very rich foods. The sugars and fats are converted to simple sugars and lactic acid in our blood which has the effect of acidifying the blood. The bugs (micro-organisms) who love this environment will thrive within it. We start to feel sick because the bugs are roaming freely through our bodies having wild parties, proliferating rapidly, and making a huge mess at our health's expense. Not good.

Get rid of the toxins and wastes

No matter how fastidious you are, at some point in your child's life, he will eat some junky stuff. It might be at a friend's birthday party, or on a sleep-over, or just something he has picked up somewhere. Don't stress over it unless it has a particularly bad effect on your child, such as an allergic reaction – swelling, rashes, localised pain – in which case you should see a doctor. If he has been eating healthy foods most of the time, the side effects (which may include vomiting, diarrhoea, a tummy rash or headache) will usually wear off after a couple of days, especially if you can feed him normally a day or so after the event. If you are at all concerned, always consult your doctor because there are some really bad diseases out there that may need urgent treatment.

The normal body temperature is 37°C (98.6°F) and an increase by one or two degrees is the body's natural response to infection. This kick starts the immune response and increases the production of white blood cells in the blood. These cells are equivalent to Special Forces troops within our bodies and we need them to fight off infections. Additionally, every one degree Centigrade rise boosts the body's basal metabolic rate by 13% and if you are sick, it may increase by 30-40% above normal.[13] The energy requirements of the body increase proportionally, so you should provide nutritious food to eat at this time. Vegetable broths or thin soups are an excellent supplement and easily digested by the sick child.

So a slight fever is good for the body's initial response to infection and shouldn't be dropped too early. With my children, I held off giving medications to counteract a fever and, instead, regularly monitored their temperature. If it started to go too high, then I took measures to drop it. These included using cool face washers or tepid baths (not currently recommended) to drop body temperature, rather than using drugs as a first step. Drugs notoriously have side effects – some quite bad – so I preferred to use more body-friendly techniques before bringing in the big guns. This also meant I spent more time caring for my sick child; something that they all appreciated. They need lots of TLC – Tender Loving Care – at this time, so keep them comfortable and as happy as possible. It's important to make the time to do this.

---

[13]   Shetty, P. *Nutrition, Immunity & Infection*, 2010: pg 23.

If you need to give your child medication, paracetamol is the preferred choice because it has fewer side-effects compared with aspirin. Aspirin should *not* be given to any child under 14 years old. With both medications, overdoses can be fatal, so always keep any medications in your home locked away and well out of reach of curious kids.

There is some excellent information from the Royal Children's Hospital in Melbourne that is available online for you to refer to if you are at all unsure.[14]

In general, if a tummy bug has been ingested, it will cause a quickening of the alimentary system and it is expelled fairly soon. Vomiting and diarrhoea often occur at the same time, so stay near a toilet and be prepared with bowls and towels if you're in a hurry. Encourage your child to sip water during this time to avoid dehydration.

> While our four children were still quite young, my husband and I took them to visit some of the western states of North America. The trip took in California, Arizona, Nevada, Utah, and Mexico. We took a bus trip to Mexico and our young son must have picked up a tummy bug sometime prior to or during the trip. To give him credit, he did try to make it to the toilet at the back of the bus. Consequently, as a *good* mother, I can't remember much of the journey because I was cleaning up the sprayed vomit in the lavatory space for nearly the entire time it took to drive to Mexico!
>
> **TIP: When travelling with kids, make sure you carry some sick bags, moist towelettes, and anti-bacterial hand cleaner.**

If the bowel feels a bit bloated or constipated, psyllium husks stirred into a glass of water and taken immediately will provide some extra fibre for the bowel muscles to push against during the contraction and relaxation of the peristalsis process. It should get things moving nicely again. There are plenty of other remedies you might like to try,[15] but if your diet is balanced, you shouldn't need to resort to anything too harsh.

To recover from an overdose of rich fatty or sweet foods, we need to eat or drink foods that will reverse their acidifying effect on the blood, rather

[14] The Royal Children's Hospital Melbourne: *Kids health info for parents* factsheet http://www.rch.org.au/kidsinfo/factsheets.cfm?doc_id=5200

[15] Jensen, B. *Dr. Jensen's Guide to Diet and Detoxification*, 2000; pg 45-59.

than popping pills to mask the symptoms. Some foods you can eat are raw tomatoes (not cooked), lemons, spinach, or red apples (Delicious or Jonathon varieties).[16] These foods help to alkalinise the blood making it less desirable for some bugs to grow, thus allowing your immune response to have the desired effect and start working on engulfing any invaders and removing them from your body through the lymphatic and circulatory systems. You know it's working if you gently feel the lymph glands (nodes) on either side of the neck, just under the jaw. If there are lumps there (possibly painful ones), then the nodes are filling up with foreign particles that have been captured and ingested by the body's white blood cells. This is great because the body is actively removing the bugs that have tried to take control of your body and have caused you to feel unwell. Another caution is if the lymph nodes become too enlarged and very painful. This could indicate a *bacterial* infection which may need antibiotic treatment. You should get your doctor's opinion if this happens.

So, be careful and aware of the foods your kids eat and of the quantities taken. Small amounts may be tolerated, but not large ones.

Did I mention to give your kids water to drink?

In cases of fever and also to speed up the healing and elimination process, water – and *only* water – should be given in small amounts (mouthfuls) *frequently* to maintain hydration levels. This cannot be emphasised enough. Dehydration of sick children is a common problem – whether it is caused by overheating from too many blankets or from a bout of diarrhoea that can quickly remove fluids from the body. Don't feed your child during these bouts as this can create further dehydration and stress to the overworked digestive system when it really needs a rest. Just provide fresh water.

Purchase food for the right reason

When you purchase food, do it for the right reason. If it's just for the weekly meals, then stay focussed on the nutritional aspects. Stick with

---

[16]   Jensen, B. *Dr. Jensen's Guide to Diet and Detoxification*, 2000; Table 6.1, pg 82-84.

fresh foods as much as possible and introduce more raw vegetables each time. If you must buy something with a label on it, read it carefully and avoid the ones with added nasties – preservatives, colourings, flavourings.[17] Buy product that contains water, carbohydrates, proteins, fats, vitamins, and minerals in proportion to your body's requirements. Foods lower in saturated fats and simple sugars (sucrose, glucose, lactose), and higher in complex carbohydrates (pasta, rice and other grains) will give you the energy you need to get through the day without popping pills and energy drinks. Just remember that the normal metabolism of the body takes about a day and a half to convert the energy sourced from good foods into glycogen[18] in your muscles ready for you to use. So, plan ahead if you know you have a big day coming up and eat the right foods at the right time for you to get the best benefit.

In preparation for the Melbourne Marathon which is usually run on a Sunday morning in the spring, there is a big carbo-load meal of pasta or rice organised on the previous Friday evening for the participants. This ensures that the energy needed to get through the big race is available at the right time.

You may find that your weekly shopping bills will be reduced as an additional benefit because raw and natural foods often cost less than pre-packaged meals and highly processed products.

If you have a party coming up, then by all means buy some treats. This is the right reason to buy this type of food. If it is an occasional event (once every two or three months), then it really is a *treat* and not something that becomes expected as part of a daily occurrence. Sometimes you will need to explain the rules about treats to your child, especially if they see other kids around them getting them all the time. It might seem a little unfair, but you are doing the best thing for your child's body as well as their mind. When your child knows the events that are worthy of a treat, then it gives them something to aim for (such as a reward for excellent work or behaviour) or to look forward to, like a birthday.

---

[17] Refer to *The Chemical Maze Shopping Companion* by Bill Statham for a list of all the chemicals that are added to foods and cosmetics.

[18] One of the body's natural energy sources.

The body can usually cope with the occasional treat as it has time to safely remove any substances that aren't that good for it. Some treats may taste really good, but once they have gone past the tongue and its taste buds, the sensation of pleasure is also gone. Many of these treats, such as lollies, have *empty* calories, which means they are providing no nutritional benefit at all, but they are full of sweeteners, flavours, and colours that are often harmful, especially in large quantities.

It comes with a caution. Your kids' bodies will be used to eating good, healthy foods, so don't over indulge on the treats too much because they may suffer some undesirable after-effects, including vomiting, sore tummies, rashes, headaches, cold symptoms, and possibly fever. The effects usually pass after a day or two when the substances have been expelled from their bodies.

When you have gone through this cycle a few times, you realise that it's not much fun, and your kids will eventually realise it too. This makes it easier for you as a parent because you don't have to explain to them why they shouldn't have something that will make them feel sick. They will hopefully have a greater appreciation of the situation and decide not to suffer in the longer term.

If you teach your children the fundamentals of good nutrition at an early age, this will set them up for the future and give them the best possible opportunity to live a long, healthy, and comfortable life.

Many of our young people are now expected to live shorter lives than their parents or grandparents because of obesity and its related illnesses, like diabetes and heart disease. This is a reversal of the previous trend where subsequent generations outlived their predecessors. If we go back a couple of generations, people may have been just as ignorant of nutrition, but food tended to be available in its natural or unprocessed form and people had to prepare and cook their own meals. The current generation of teenagers to thirty year olds have generally been misguided by food companies that have put nutrition in the bin in the chase for the mighty dollar. They tend to market their products as fast and tasty, so they disguise any negative qualities of their product with the reduced effort it takes to acquire the so-called meal.

FOOD FOR THOUGHT

In the United States of America, about one-quarter of the adult population visits a fast food restaurant every day.[19] The trend in Australia is to follow the USA, so we will probably be in a similar situation at some point in the near future. This statistic is frightening because if we extrapolate to another 20 or 30 years, we will have a forecast for ill-health and early mortality.

At the time of writing, in Australia we have a population that is just over 22.3 million people and an adult population (15+ years) of 81.1% or 18.08 million.[20] One-quarter of the adult population adds up to a little over 4.5 million people and if these people eat fast food every day, then it is not unreasonable to assume that over 4.5 million people will be expected to suffer needless ill-health or early death over the next two or three decades. This is equivalent to the population of the entire state of Queensland.

A sobering thought.

When you purchase fresh produce, prepare your own food, and teach your kids how to do it, then you will enjoy good health and emotional and mental balance because you have to slow down and share the experience with those you love.

See your General Practitioner (GP) if you're unsure

As a parent, many of us feel as if we shouldn't *bother* our local doctor (GP) with our concerns:

He'll think we're over-protective or paranoid about our child.

This is a myth! Part of your job as a parent is to be on the lookout for your child and if you are ever unsure about his health, do not hesitate to visit your GP, no matter how trivial it may seem. Find a GP in whom you have absolute trust and build a good relationship with him or her. Your GP's job is to help

---

[19]   Schlosser, Eric. *Fast Food Nation*, 2002: pg 3.

[20]   Australian Bureau of Statistics website: *www.abs.gov.au/AUSSTATS/abs@.nsf/ mf/3101.0* updated Dec 2010.

you and your child to stay healthy or get well again, and he or she is more than willing to set your mind at ease. It is far better to be safe, than sorry!

A thermometer is one of those small, but indispensible, instruments that must be in every home. In earlier days, the narrow glass ones that you had to shake the mercury down before sticking it under your tongue were often hard to read – especially if you needed reading glasses. Choosing one with a large, clear digital readout makes it easier and more accurate to read. Just ensure you know how to use it and where to use it *before* you need to use it. Practice which button to push and place it under your child's armpit. Hold it for the required amount of time – usually the thermometer will beep rapidly or have a continuous beep when it is done. Checking how it works when your child is well helps to give you some comfort because you will know how to do it when you're under pressure. It also teaches your child that there are times when they have to be still for a few minutes, that it is not going to hurt them, and that it makes a funny noise. The armpit is the most suitable place for kids of all ages, though older kids can have the thermometer placed under their tongue, as they can be told not to chew on it.

In the following situations, you need to take your child to your GP:[21]

1. If a fever or high temperature (above 41°C or 105.8°F) is still present after an hour of home treatment.
2. If your child is less than three months of age and he has a temperature of 38.5°C or 101.3°F.
3. If your child is between three months and one year of age and his fever has lasted longer than 24 hours.
4. If the fever has not improved in 72 hours (three days).
5. If the fever has lasted more than five days.
6. If these symptoms exist with a fever: stiff neck; light hurting his eyes (photophobia); vomiting; rash; breathing difficulties; feeling in pain; more sleepy than usual; and not wanting to drink.

In all other situations where your child is unwell, if you've had previous experience with it, then do what must be done, even if that means seeing your GP or specialist. If you don't know what to do, a simple call or visit to your GP will point you in the right direction.

---

[21] Fries, J.F., Vickery, D.M., Telford, R.D. & Reid R.A. *Take Care of Yourself* Australian Edition, 2001: pg 210-211.

4

Simplicity or No Dramas

Keep things simple and in perspective.

Instructions:

1. Read the Introduction.
2. Deal with CHANGE calmly.
3. Avoid the soap operas of life.
4. The brain needs stimulation.
5. Keep it Super Simple (KISS principle).

Something you definitely need to consider is the creation of drama in your life – or rather, the lack of it. Many people thrive on making *mountains out of molehills*. Or another justification commonly used is that they are only thinking of the *worst case scenario* so they can plan for it. I agree with planning for the worst, but many people stay in that space and forget to *hope for the best*. If you are always thinking of the worst case, guess what you will attract into your life. The worst case! This is counter-productive for a good parent and can teach unwanted and unnecessary behavioural patterns in your child.

When my kids were in Year 5 at school, one of the projects undertaken was to create a pioneer's home. Each child could choose their own style of home – mud-brick cottage; timber Queenslander with a verandah all the way around; blue stone house; grassy lean-to; lighthouse; and so on.

This project could be done at home, and it was truly inspiring to see the *creations* that came back to school on the due date. I was amazed to see how talented some 10 year olds were because their houses were like architectural models! (Obviously, mum and/or dad were heavily involved in the project as well.)

The concept of involving the parents in the design and construction was a good idea even though some took it to the extreme. Some parents were too scared to let their child carry it for fear of dropping the masterpiece, or because it was too heavy. Also, it wasn't hard to see the homes that were built only by the child; they were very rough and simple.

Whether the topic is a model home or a solution to a problem that has cropped up in your child's life, as a parent, being involved is excellent, but after showing your child the way to do it or solve it, you need to step away and let him do it to the best of his ability – even if it's not perfect. The simpler you design a model or lay down the steps to a solution, the easier it will be to create or re-create it.

I have always been a great admirer of Jane Austen's writing and her classic novel *Pride and Prejudice* elegantly depicts the folly of humanity when it is allowed to pursue wholly narcissistic endeavours that are often exaggerated and over-dramatised. In this novel, the hero (Mr Fitzwilliam Darcy) starts out being very proud and aloof, and the heroine (Elizabeth Bennett) is willing to make judgements about people, which are quite valid in some cases, and not so valid in others. Her biggest judgement is against Darcy, and after painfully recognising her error, falls in love and marries him. Most of their acquaintance are less complicated characters; either nice and sweet, like her sister Jane; loud and bombastic, like her mother and sister Lydia; over-controlling, like Lady Catherine de Bourgh; Wickham, the womaniser; or Mr Collins, the pompous parson. The more subtle endeavours of Darcy and Elizabeth needed to undergo a material change of attitude before they could achieve their ambitions – him to lose his pride and her to lose her prejudice. They needed to learn that harsh judgements about other people were not necessarily in their best interests and that giving people the benefit of the doubt and forgiving them – or ignoring – their little foibles was a better option. The other *dramatic* characters appeared to miss their life lessons entirely, and carried on regardless down their sorry paths without so much as a second glance. This was their big mistake – don't let it be yours.

Deal with CHANGE calmly

There is an expression that states, "There are only two certainties in life – death and taxes". I would like to add a third – CHANGE. Like the other two, change occurs at any time, everyday, everywhere, with no exception. So why do most of us freak out when it occurs and have no mechanism for dealing with it rationally or calmly. There are a couple of reasons why this occurs. Firstly, we are not taught to accept and cope with change at an early age, and secondly, many people appear to thrive on the dramas of life (life's changeability) and don't really want to learn to be able to cope with it. How many of us have friends who are just itching to tell everyone the latest gossip about someone? Many of the glossy magazines and news broadcasters make money by selling stories of change in the lives of famous people. Whether a story is true, who knows? Much of it is fabricated just to sell it. Who really cares? Not many, outside of the gullible public who spend money to buy it.

It is only after a few years (or decades) before we start to see the premature aging effect this way of thinking and behaving can have on a person.

Get used to it – change occurs, so accept it as a normal part of life and as calmly as you can.

Avoid the soap operas of life

Many people are obsessed by the soap operas on TV, but I have never understood that fascination. The same thing occurs in each situation, but with a slightly different colouring. In these dramas, someone is either getting into some sort of trouble, is already in trouble, or is just getting out of trouble. The formula is the same, and yet people still watch with anticipation for the outcome of which they already know the answer. This can have a very dulling effect on the brain and its processing ability. Also, the examples shown by the actors in these soaps are not necessarily the ones that you would want to follow, as they tend to be full of over-reactions that have nothing to do with just bad acting and directing.

Strangely enough, many people follow the same troubled logic in their daily lives. An event becomes blown out of proportion to its real effect and often the reason is based on some form of guilt trip that the perpetrator (the one exaggerating it) wishes to have over the instigator (the one who did it, or made it happen in the first place). This has a very negative result and can create an environment of stress, mistrust, dislike, and antagonism between those involved and with their family or friends.

My kids were in their pre-teen years when we moved into a quiet cul-de-sac-like street with only local traffic in a mainly working class suburban area. The neighbours were generally friendly and the local kids mingled and played with ours very well. Some of the families lived together with their grandparents, so there were three generations living in the same house. I think this can be a great idea as it provides care for the elderly, as well as a ready baby sitter when the parents need some time-out. But, there are some disadvantages.

One family were very friendly and co-existed well with the other neighbours and kids, but the grandparents seemed to enjoy finding issues with everyone else. These issues may well have been there to some small extent, but often they were made worse by the behaviour of the grandparents.

On one occasion, while I was home and working inside the house, my son and some of the other kids in the street were playing outside on the road, making smiley faces in the bitumen using a highly flammable substance. The first I knew about it was when the police knocked on my door.

The grandmother had been observing the kids for at least half an hour and instead of asking them what they were doing, or coming over and asking me to find out what they were doing and stop it (like a rational person might do), she was apparently in fear for her life and called the police. Was she waiting for something terrible to happen to one of them? And then when it didn't, she decided to create another dramatic scene by calling the police. She even called the local Council and a few days later they came to clean up the road. Maybe she didn't like smiley faces.

The little respect that I had for her completely disintegrated.

I also realised that kids can get up to mischief right under your nose. Sometimes it can be serious, and other times not. In this case, no one was hurt, but if I had known about it, I would have stopped it.

If you really want to live life as a drama, please consider the unresolved issues, and unnecessary stress and anxiety you will create. This is neither an ideal existence, nor an environment for balanced and happy kids growing up. You're sending them the message that making wild assumptions and taking irrational actions are the norm. This is not, and should never be, the case.

A dad was comforting his adult daughter over the phone one day, assuring her that she will be alright and not to be upset:

You cannot be sacked because of what has happened; it is only your car window not working; they have found someone to replace you for your shift; everything is fine, so don't be upset; I will fix your car when I get home after work, and you will be able to go to work tomorrow; they can't sack you because you were sick last week; that's only your mother jumping to the worst case scenario; it's not going to happen; don't be upset; they cannot sack you legally...

He later told me that his daughter had been really sick the previous week with the flu and that one of the electric windows on her car had fallen down and wouldn't go back up. This meant it would not be secure if she went to work. He usually caught the train to work, but this day he decided to drive, otherwise, his daughter could have used his car. And, unfortunately, his wife had a tendency to jump to the worst possible conclusion whenever anything happened. This only served to upset his daughter and make her feel insecure about her job, as well as her car.

This patient dad then had to spend time consoling and comforting his distraught daughter, when it could have been avoided entirely.

If people know how to resolve problems at an early stage, they can prevent something worse from possibly happening. Thinking ahead and considering the consequences of your actions and inactions can help you decide on a sensible course to take and one with less stress to others.

A sequence of events can occur to create a situation that can be seen as good or bad or somewhere in between. How each of us reacts to that situation can tip the balance to one side or the other. In the example above, the clear facts were the car window was not working; there was no other car available to use; the daughter couldn't get to work. She had called her work to let them know the situation and they had found a replacement. Their problem was solved. Next problem – fix the car window. Her dad was going to fix it when he got home – problem solved. End of story.

If you lay it out clearly just using the facts at hand, there is no need to bring in the emotional baggage that so many people feel is necessary. This mother loves her daughter, but do you think she was helping her by making her feel so insecure about her job; telling her she was going to be sacked? Of course not! Suddenly the daughter's mind is full of thoughts of lack and insecurity: *Can they really sack me for being absent? What will I do then? How will I pay my bills? Where will I find a new job?*...

All these unnecessary thoughts are churning through her mind, causing stress and fear – the same stuff from which disease arises. It may interest you to know that this young lady (still living at home) was very ill as a child and had been given sulphur-based drugs to relieve her condition. Eventually, after many years of tests, trial, and error, it was discovered that she had a sulphur allergy. Some foods gave her really bad stomach pain, so she still needs to be very careful with her diet and avoid all foods with sulphur-based preservatives, such as sulphur dioxide in dried fruits and many other foods.

I cannot help but wonder whether growing up in an environment of stress and fear, brought on by the mother's preferred method of handling problems (over-reacting and concocting highly unlikely scenarios), may have contributed to her condition as well. I don't blame the mother – that was her training from her parents and life experiences – but at some point in an adult's life, a choice needs to be made whether to take the path of fear and excessive stress, or the path of clarity and relief. It's your decision.

If you practice making a drama out of every little thing in your life, what do you think you're going to do when something really serious happens? You'll probably go into some form of panic and be about as useful as a bowl of quivering jelly. So, when something unusual happens in your life – small or big – don't over-react. Stay calm and simply *observe* what is happening. It is only from a place of calmness that you can find a quick solution that is based on rational and logical thought.

The brain needs stimulation

Ask any mum or dad who has been at home for a while – and this could be years caring for babies and children – what changes happen to them if they return to the workforce. Suddenly their brains open up and expand and they may feel like they have been released from some form of hibernation or suspension during the time spent as the primary carer for young children.

Caring for children can be incredibly stimulating and satisfying but this depends on the individual carer (mum or dad) and their instincts or training. It is a job that is also extremely repetitive and it is this repetition that leads the brain to shut down and become less responsive over time.

Recent research has shown that physical exercise increases the production of stem cells in the brain and that if the brain is then stimulated by challenging activities, the stem cells are used to produce active nerve cells in the brain.[22],[23] If no associated mental stimulation occurs after the physical exercise, then the stem cells become reabsorbed by the body and disintegrate into nothing.

This is fantastic news not only for stroke victims and others who have suffered any brain disorders or damage, but also for parents and their kids. Now I understand why I always felt better and could process my work as a computer programmer with greater clarity on the days when I had done some form of physical exercise in the morning prior to going to work.

In addition, the work of neuroplasticians has discovered that the brain is not fixed as was once thought, but is extremely changeable and capable of incredible growth and healing to by-pass damaged cells and

[22]   *Catalyst*, Australian Broadcasting Corporation (ABC) Television, 7 October 2010.
[23]   Doidge N., *The Brain That Changes Itself*, 2007, pgs 245-257.

tissues given the right treatment and activities.[24] People have been able to recover from what were once considered unrecoverable afflictions, such as Obsessive Compulsive Disorder (OCD); Cerebral Palsy; paralysis and speech disability as a result of stroke; age-related brain loss; sensory loss of hearing, sight, and balance; learning difficulties; and many other brain disorders.

In my view, this means we have no excuses anymore. It all goes back to what we think about and how we apply it.

Many people believe that plonking their kid in front of the TV or buying them a computer is enough. Sorry to burst the bubble, but it's not. A computer is merely a useful tool and it is wasted on young kids – they only need some basic toys and their imaginations. Older kids who know how to use the computer properly should be made aware that it is only a tool and not a companion, even though it can be a play thing with amazing graphical capabilities or a channel with which to communicate with the world. Parents should make themselves available to help guide their child around the internet and teach them the pitfalls as well as the strengths of this amazing tool. If you don't know it, get some help to learn it. You'll be doing both of you a favour.

Nothing can substitute for the face-to-face interactions that create a balanced social being; one who is brave enough to meet the unknown head on and willing to risk some emotional injury as he learns to deal with people on a myriad of levels. Kids of all ages need to learn good social skills – how to play together happily, whether in a team or individually; how to share community equipment fairly; and how to deal with others who don't know the same rules.

In general, kids love physical activity – whether it's playing with a bat and ball; building castles in a sand pit or down the beach; playing hide and seek; or chasing the pet dog. All of these activities are stimulating and fun. You can enjoy it too, just by joining in and going with the flow. The emphasis is on *physical*. The large muscle groups need to be working and moving together for this to work. This means the leg muscles, and in particular the thigh (quadriceps) and hamstring muscles behind the thighs. Later on, you may introduce other mentally stimulating activities that are more passive, but at this point, the *active* in activity is all important.

---

[24] Doidge N., *The Brain That Changes Itself*, 2007, pgs 132-163.

Keep it Super Simple (KISS principle)

No matter what you do with your kids, stick with the KISS principle. Keep things as simple as possible. Resist the temptation to over-control the activity or play, or to try and make a project out of it. Kids love spontaneity and simplicity, and quality time with your kids should be just that – simple and spontaneous.

If you get out the paints and brushes, make sure you have an area that is already easy to clean up because it's going to get messy. The parent who sits at their child's elbow ready to jump into action as soon as the first drop is spilled is going to freak out the child and eventually he will want to stop the activity simply because mum or dad is making it impossible for him to have fun – no spontaneity. He may also change the focus of the activity from creating a painting to seeing how freaked out mum or dad can get if he splashes paint everywhere. That's his idea of creating a spontaneous activity.

Instead, simply observe your child and ensure he is doing appropriate things with the tools in hand – not drinking the paint, or trying to give the pet pooch a new hairdo in red or purple. It may liven up the dog, but it is inappropriate behaviour, and kids need to know the boundaries from as young an age as possible.

Set up your own area, too and do the task alongside your child. Then work individually for a while and compare your creations after five or ten minutes. Resist the temptation to tell your child what to do. Let him create all by himself and encourage his efforts using phrases like:

That's fantastic, Johnny. I really love the colours/ shapes/ patterns.

Well done, Sarah. That's looking really colourful/ brilliant/ stripy/ dotty/ imaginative.

If your child asks for help, then by all means, help him. This situation is different because your child has initiated the help, not you. But rather than completing the entire picture for your kid, show him an option (one at a time so he isn't confused) and let him try it for himself. If he doesn't like it, then try to find him another way. Keep doing this until he finds something he likes, or you run out of ideas. If he has had enough of that activity, then pack it up even if the masterpiece is unfinished.

When a child has had enough of something, you need to be aware of that fact and do something about it as soon as possible. Ignoring it will just create unwanted drama in your life because little Johnny will start throwing things around to get your attention. There's another old saying I like: *A stitch*

41

in time, saves nine. This can refer to mending clothes as well as to dealing with a situation promptly to avoid a much larger mess. Never ignore your kids, because the underlying message you are sending them is that they aren't important enough for you. They will then do something to make you notice them, and it's amazing how often this occurs in a public place. How many times have you seen a child throwing a tantrum in a supermarket? Probably more than enough times, just like the rest of us.

If you can focus on keeping your life as simple and uncomplicated as possible; staying as calm as you can under most conditions and situations; then your home life will be as peaceful as it can be in this 21st century where it is often commented that no one seems to find the time to be polite or to just say a gentle hello.

5

Rights and Responsibilities

*Kids have rights and with those
right come responsibilities.*

Instructions:

1. Read the Introduction.
2. Learn the rules.
3. The first rule is respect for all.
4. Respect and obey the rules.
5. The rights of parenthood.
6. The responsibilities of parenthood.
7. The rights of childhood.
8. The responsibilities of childhood.

Like it or not, we live in a society that is governed by rules. Some people think that rules are annoying and made to be broken, but that is a very selfish viewpoint. Just think of the chaos that would ensue if we had no road rules and everyone drove anywhere on the road and ignored the traffic signals. We wouldn't get very far, would we? There would be some people thinking this is great fun, laughing and weaving around the roads like a misguided spider's web. Then a whole bunch of confused people might be scratching their heads in utter disbelief with no idea how to solve the mess or reach their destinations. Meanwhile, the vast majority of people might be highly annoyed and wondering why no one is paying attention to the rules. We need rules to maintain a degree of control over our *social environment*. When you learn to accept that fact, then they don't appear to be half as bad as what you once thought.

Learn the rules

Unless you live in the outback, where you have so much room to move that you can make your own rules, you need to abide by the local laws of your community and your society's rules and expectations. This is what organised people, societies, and nations do. If you don't, then you end up incarcerated, excommunicated or worse. So, play by the rules and your life will be a little less chaotic.

For your child to be able to play by the rules, he needs to learn them first. Hopefully, you, as the parent, have spent some time in your current community, so you have a good idea what the rules are and can teach them to your child. Teach him best by your good example; with positive encouragement for his right actions and right words; and with love, respect, and good humour throughout. This topic is covered further in another chapter.

If you don't know your local laws and rules, then you need to seek help from community-minded groups and government organisations, such as the police, trusted friends or your local library. Seek assistance whenever you need it and it will be forthcoming if you are humble and show gratitude. There are many people – from kids to adults – who try to get help or knowledge while maintaining a superior attitude of *I already know everything!* Not surprisingly, this only seems to attract blockages, false information, and unfriendly responses. By changing their attitude to a softer, more respectful approach, these people are far more likely to attract and be helped by someone with a considerate nature and a willingness to be of service.

The first rule is respect for all

Before your child learns the laws specific to a particular area or community, the *first* rule to learn that covers anywhere, anybody, and anytime is RESPECT. Respect is all-encompassing because it applies to everybody and everything. Everybody has a right to be respected and treated with dignity as a human being. This is a fundamental birthright and at some point in our lives, sooner or later, we recognise this.

If you treat people with respect, then you are more likely to get respect in return. Unfortunately, this is not guaranteed for all occasions because some people have yet to learn how to treat people respectfully at any time. Even so, this does not mean that you can then mistreat someone else. One bad experience doesn't give you the right to be bad too. You are a better person if you remain calm and polite under pressure – easier said, than done, I know, but it's definitely worth the effort – so practice it every time.

Sometimes we feel like we have to fight for the respect that's owed to us if we feel it is being degraded – *How dare my son talk to me like that? I don't deserve to be treated like that! After all I've done for him! He* owes *me respect!*

I'm sure many of us have felt that way at some time, but if we stop and think about it, why do we feel so indignant? Yes, the respect is missing, but what has occurred to make that happen? What have we done to lose it? Yes, I do mean us – the parents. Sometimes you might be able to pick a time and a place when something relatively big happened; when there was a disagreement between yourself and your child, and after that time a degree of respect was lost. If nothing is done at that time to heal the emotional wounds, then the respect you once had that might relate to that event or subject is gone – maybe not forever, but for a very long time.

Our family used to go down the beach every summer season to sail at our favourite yacht club. As I was the youngest of the family, I was the last to learn how to sail and spent many hours playing in the sand.

In those days, my mother used to make a picnic lunch with all the trimmings and kept it all neatly together in an esky.

One day, before everyone left the beach to start the sailing race, I decided to tie our dog to the handle of the esky to stop him from chasing the boats.

Well, you can guess what happened – the sailors took off, the dog took off, and so did the esky; spilling it's neatly packed contents all over the sand.

My mother was livid; she was understandably so angry that she tore strips off me right then and there, in front of everybody.

I was so embarrassed and humiliated that I hid under a towel for the rest of the afternoon. Some people came up to me later to try and coax me out, but all they said was to stop being silly; and that nobody else cared about it. Reinforcing my feelings of abject failure, they missed the point entirely.

I cared about it. I did something really stupid, but I felt so utterly humiliated that I can still feel the stinging emotional pain decades later. I don't know if my mother actually forgave me for doing that - all her hard work and effort gone to waste. She did forget about it and went on with life, but I couldn't get out of that 'unforgiven' space for a very long time. At the time, I would have liked her to give me a big hug and tell me that she forgave me for doing such a silly thing, and that it wasn't a complete disaster; and that some food was edible, but it didn't happen. I guess she was too angry with me to do it at the time, and then afterwards it was too late to consider doing.

I learned more than one thing that day: never to tie the dog to a food box; but also, if I ever make a mistake in front of my mother, be prepared to be humiliated.

Can you see, from a child's point of view, how some respect for a mother might be lost in this situation even though it was entirely the child's fault? Think about your own experiences as a child, and maybe as a parent. Did you have something like this happen to you?

If you were the child, then hold an image of your parent in your mind and forgive him or her completely. Visualise yourself giving your parent a big hug and a kiss and saying that you are sorry for making him angry and that you love him and forgive him for causing you to feel distressed and humiliated.

If you were the parent, then visualise yourself hugging and kissing your child; telling him you are sorry for getting angry and upset, and causing him to feel distressed and humiliated; and that you forgive him completely and love him dearly.

After you have done the visualisation enough times for you to really feel the love and forgiveness completely and comfortably, then go to the person in your visualisation (if they are still alive) and do the same thing in reality. The visualisation process changes your attitude towards them and helps it come to pass because the old negative patterns have been cleared away and replaced by a positive and loving pattern.

If the person is no longer alive, still do the visualisation process because it helps you to clear the bad pattern, so you won't repeat it with someone else. It also helps you to feel more comfortable about the original event and to be able to forgive yourself as much as the other person. If you do it properly, you will feel a sense of relief.

Respect and obey the rules

Teach your child to play by the rules, not only in the games he plays with other kids, but also in all his daily interactions. This is one of the most important lessons you can pass on to your child. It is an *investment* in his future because you are teaching him a vital life skill; one that will stand him in good stead no matter where his life's journey takes him.

When a person is content to follow the rules, then he knows that he is being fair. That's what rules are supposed to do – metaphorically and actually, they level out the playing field for everyone who participates – in a footy match, or the game of life.

Another old saying I particularly like is: *It's not whether you win or lose, it's how you play the game.* Unfortunately, over the last few years (decades) the emphasis on winning (or not being a loser) seems to have predominated the thoughts and actions of not only many great sporting athletes, but also the average Joe Blow. Winning at all costs – no matter what the consequences – has taken over the thoughts and strategies of the players, coaches, promoters, and management.

The exaggerated payments made to the winners are almost obscene and often appear totally out of proportion to the achievement. This imbalance towards the top-end has placed all emphasis on the ultimate goal of winning, and completely ignored the main reason for doing the activity in the first place – the love of participation. How many athletes have lost all credibility and integrity because they have taken performance-enhancing drugs just to help them win; in spite of the consequences. Many suffer serious health issues now because of their poor choices in the past. How incredibly stupid! Now they are seen to be cheats and are excluded from playing their favourite sport. Even if they swear off all drugs and complete rehabilitation programs, their sporting life will never be what it once was – it is tarnished forever.

If these people had kept their focus on a participation based on fairness and honesty, and did the best they could given their talent and wholesome training, they would still be enjoying the game (life) as well as being able to hold their head high in public. They would still be trusted. Often this competitiveness can be taught in schools, so if you see these traits being mirrored by your child after a period of time in the school environment, question their actions and encourage them to think about what they are learning and to always act rationally, not like an automaton.

So, play the game by the rules and live your life fairly.

The rights of parenthood

You have the right to look after and care for your child to the best of your ability. This world is made up of a mosaic of colourful people and places. Each of us has a unique heritage and environment to offer our kids and, I believe, from a spiritual level, they choose us as their parents because of the life lessons we can give them. Every one of us has an idea of how we want to bring up our kids and these are based on our own unique mix of cultural, spiritual, educational, and experiential interactions. These give us direction and purpose in our lives and it is completely understandable for any given parent to want to build these same values and morals in their children. Whether you are rich or poor, ignorant or educated, your success as a parent is totally independent of these things. The main tools you need are unconditional love and respect and these can be felt by anyone; there is no cultural or class distinction attached to them, so any parent, from any walk of life, can express them.

You have the right to make mistakes. You do *not* have the right to *dwell* on them. We all make mistakes – that's part of being human. As a parent, you will make the same mistakes that millions before you have done, and what millions after you will do. Learn from them, forgive yourself for making them, and move on to a more aware and appreciative place.

You have the right to feel a vast array of emotions, such as, anger, guilt, confusion, hopelessness, sadness, concern, loss, acceptance, joy, happiness, pride, and immense love. Your children will help you feel some of them, and quite probably, all of them. When they come, stay as calm as you can be given the situation to evoke such feelings, and remember that whether the feeling is good or bad, it will come and then it will go. They all pass with time.

You do *not* have the right to *worry*. Many people waste so much time and energy worrying about their kids. Don't do it. If you break it down; what is worry? When you worry about someone or something, you are putting yourself in a place of uncertainty and misery. This causes you unnecessary stress and makes you feel bad. You're not actually doing anything except thinking about all the things that can go wrong and working yourself into an anxious mood where you might feel sick and unable to rest or sleep. By doing this, you are focussing on these events happening and that focus is making them more *likely* to happen. So, I repeat, do not worry, it's really bad for you and your kids.

Some people confuse *worry* with being *concerned*. There is a huge difference. Worry is a totally negative and useless energy because it achieves nothing – unless your objective is to become a paranoid freak running around after your kid making him nervous and insecure! *Concern*, on the other hand, allows you to prepare for future events and mitigate, to the best of your ability, any potentially negative thing that might crop up from time to time, such as making sure your kid uses a bike helmet to prevent a broken skull if he falls off his bike.

Help your kids to see the consequences of their actions beforehand, and to plan for their goals and ambitions, no matter how small or big. Be pro-active, not in-active (by worrying) or re-active (by over dramatising events).

The responsibilities of parenthood

It is your responsibility to be loving, fair, and consistent with *all* your children. Treat all your children equally; play no favourites and an environment where resentment and bitterness could grow should be avoided. Children notice things, and even if you think you're being clever and secretive, your body language and tone of voice will betray your thoughts and feelings. Favouritism will also create resentment between your children and that is a sad legacy to leave to the next generation. Parents should want all their children to love and care for each other; to be able to share life's journey as companions, confidantes, and trusted support in good and bad times. You will not be around forever to look out for your kids, so help to provide them with a foundation of familial support and love upon which they can rely.

It is your responsibility to *learn* from the mistakes you have made so that you don't repeat them. How many times have you done it yourself or you've seen other people repeat the same mistake again and again? Obviously, the lesson has not been learned. So, when something happens to you (often a bad thing), take a backseat and observe the whole scene. What has just happened here? How did it start, how did it escalate, and how did it end? Now think of a different scenario for the middle and ending, given that the same beginning must occur. If you stop and think long enough, you will usually be able to see where things went awry and how you can change it so it doesn't happen in the future. That is the lesson! The more times you stop and consider events, the easier it becomes to see the right, or at least the less painful, way to handle something.

It is your responsibility to be *unconditional* in all your dealings with each child. Show them the joy you feel simply because they are there with you. In your mind, tear up any unwritten contracts you may want to hold over your children, because your kids don't know they exist. Do all your daily tasks (yes, even the drudge ones) freely and with a feeling of gratitude that you have the ability to do them. There are many people in the world who have disabilities which prevent them from doing even the most menial tasks. They need to rely on someone else to help them every single day. How do you think they would feel if they heard you complaining about your lot in life – what a drag to have to do all the dishes, or wash all the clothes, or take out the rubbish? Wouldn't they be ecstatic just to be able to stand up out of their wheelchairs and walk! Really *feel* gratitude for all the abilities you have now – they are a gift.

Additionally, you should not do anything for anyone else with the impression that they will be unrealistically appreciative of what you have done for them. Many times we place too much emphasis on what we have done for others, and not really taken much notice about what they have done for us. On the tally board in our minds, we chalk up all the things we have done for them, for which they need to show us eternal gratitude! The couple of minor things they have done for us begrudgingly get chalked up on the tally board just to *prove* we are fair. It appears that in reality, most of us chalk up many more marks for ourselves than for the others around us. Even your teenager generally believes that he does too much for you, and if he doesn't, he still has to put up with your constant nagging, which is worth many marks. How many mothers are out there trying to play the *guilt* card on their family: *I've worked so hard to clean the house, do the washing and ironing, cook the meals, and feed the dog!* The guilt-ridden family has not necessarily asked for so much special treatment. After all, it is your job. Remember, you wanted it in the first place, so accept your own choices and the lessons they bring to your life.

Wouldn't it be nice to just wipe the board clean? Think about how relieving and liberating that would be. So what's stopping you? The only one who cares about the tally board is yourself, so erase it and chop up the board so you can't go back to it again. Visualise it in your mind's eye and make it really vivid. Use your imagination to smash it to bits – go on, have a bit of fun with it. No one is going to get hurt by it. On the contrary, you will feel much happier and lighter. Accept the tasks that are presented to you with a real sense of happiness and gratitude. Life should not be miserable; it should be joyful, so do your bit to make it happen for yourself.

It is your responsibility to set the boundaries for acceptable behaviour from your kids and not budge from them. Many people can tolerate the poor behaviour of their own kids, but other people won't be so patient. They will shun them and tell them to go away because they are being rude. If you want your kids to be loved and respected by the people in the community that nurtures you, then you need to make sure they are worthy of it. Their behaviour reflects your skills as a parent, so do the best job of it that you can. Your kids need to know how to behave in different situations, such as, when using public transport – offer your seat to a lady, or elderly person, who may be standing; when in the classroom – always listen to the teacher, be respectful, and do your best to learn well; while at home – do all your chores before going out to play and help out around the place whenever you can; at a party – laugh and have fun, but look out for your friends, especially if they have had too much to drink. All these types of expectations need to be shown and told to your kids so they know what to do. They don't pick it up by osmosis (through the pores of their skin), so you must teach it to them until they are old enough to learn for themselves. Set your own boundaries, and if there is a disagreement between mum and dad with some of them, work out a compromise with which both of you are content.

Recently, there were two separate occasions when I was impressed by the behaviour of some boys who were with a group of their school friends.

On the first occasion, I was using a pay machine to pay for a car park. It was situated opposite a lift and a group of school boys were just entering the lift. Before the door closed, one of the young lads politely asked me if I wanted to use the lift. I said no thanks, but I also thanked him for asking me, because that doesn't happen very often.

On the second occasion, I was on a train and observed a couple of school kids waiting to get off at the next station. They started to move out the doorway, but then stepped back to make room for an elderly couple who were also disembarking.

Again, I was very impressed with these young people who showed such an awareness of the needs of the people around them. They put their own needs *after* those of someone else. Too often these days we see quite the reverse. It was wonderful to observe such respect for others in action.

It is your responsibility to *discipline* your child. Both parents must agree to any discipline and behavioural expectations. If you don't, then your kid may play one parent off from the other. This leads to situations where the child has asked one parent if he can do something and that parent says no. He then asks the other parent, who says yes. So he goes ahead and does it, to the annoyance of the first parent. A disagreement between the parents now starts, while the child is laughing to himself about how clever he is in tricking his parents. This is an unacceptable situation, so be prepared and avoid it. Discipline is necessary for when a child starts to push the limits of the boundaries set by the parents. If no disciplinary steps are taken at that time (and *every* other time it happens), then the child is doomed to become the intolerable spoilt brat who we all know and abhor. Do not put your child in this position, because he will have few friends and the ones he does have are probably only going to use him up for whatever things he can give them, such as money or trinkets.

If your child oversteps a boundary, then you must be ready with a suitable disciplinary measure (punishment). No matter what the civil libertarians might exclaim, you must have some forms of punishment ready to go in your parental toolbox (figuratively speaking). In general, you will not need to use any serious punishment while your child is under three or four, but every situation is different. Babies are usually happy when they are clean, fed, and well rested, so in general there are few disciplinary problems here. Toddlers are free-roaming spirits, so they can unknowingly get into trouble. In the early years, it's not usually intentional, as much as curiosity running amok, so damage-control is needed more than anything else, and this may include some discipline when a boundary is being tested. It's when they become a little bit older and they have observed the behaviour of people around them from all walks of life, and hence, are more attune with worldly ways, that some alternative methods of changing their minds and behaviour may become necessary.

When a young toddler is in the home, many people use cupboard door and drawer locks – especially in their kitchens – to help keep curious fingers and hands out of places they should not enter.

I can remember feeling a little irritated whenever I visited family or friends and tried to open a cupboard or drawer. The locks kept on getting in the way; sometimes causing me to hurt my own fingers.

When we had children of our own, we also put locks on some of the cupboards, but only on the necessary ones, such as the cupboard under the sink where chemicals and harsh detergents were kept.

By the time our third and fourth babies arrived, we had 'proofed' the house so much that we didn't need to put any locks on any of the cupboards or drawers. All the chemicals and potential poisons were put into a high cupboard in the laundry which was always closed off when I wasn't washing clothes.

In the kitchen, we had one cupboard and one drawer (the lowest) specifically designed for the toddlers. They held non-breakable things like plastic utensils, plates, tumblers, containers, and lids; and pots and pans. The kids were shown the cupboard and drawer they could use and were told not to open the other ones because there were heavy and breakable plates and crockery that we needed to use for eating and when we have dinner parties. Once they could see the things in there and felt their weight, it helped give them an appreciation of why they couldn't play with them. Glass and sharp objects were kept up high out of harm's way.

Each child loved to play with the things in 'their' cupboard and drawer and, apart from a bit of a mess at times, the kitchen was relatively safe. The biggest lesson I found was that each child developed a sense of responsibility for the more delicate things that we used on a daily basis. Our table crockery has lasted many decades.

> When other children came to visit, we had to be more vigilant until they knew the rules of the kitchen, too.
>
> If anyone ignored the rules, they suffered the consequences. We played no favourites and everyone who was naughty was given the same punishment.

It often starts with the *naughty corner* – where the child must go and sit in a special corner reserved for such a punishment. He is not allowed to move from that spot for, say, five minutes, but that is dependant upon the naughty deed he has done. For example, if he has refused to pack up his toys, then five minutes in the naughty corner without any toys, books, or amusements, might be enough to change his mind. If he has kicked the dog, then that is much worse, he may need to be 10 minutes in the naughty corner or possibly facing the brick wall – solid walls aren't damaged by a petulant toddler or younger pre-teen. During these times, you must remain strong and never give in to the wailing child. If you do, it will be much harder to discipline your child next time. Keep a watchful eye on him, but don't give in. Be seen to be doing your usual tasks, so that he doesn't think he can use it as an attention-seeking ritual. Other punishments include excluding the child from something that is important to him, such as a favourite TV program, some special play time with friends, or with mum or dad.

The pre-teens and teenagers who misbehave require a more mature approach to discipline and punishment. Again, restricting the use of a cherished item, such as a computer, modem (or the connecting wire), cable TV, or *grounding* them, can be enough to produce the desired change in attitude. Sometimes they don't really know why they are misbehaving, but often it can correlate pretty highly with their recent exposure to other kids (younger or older) who misbehave regularly. This is more obvious in younger kids, or in those with a more gullible personality that allows them to be easily led into trouble. This is why it is important to know the type of friends with whom your child interacts. If they are good kids, then they won't generally initiate a direction that leads to trouble. If your child does have some friends who are used to doing their own thing without any consequences, then you should sit down with your child in a relaxed setting and talk to him about their behaviour and whether he knows why they behave that way. Painting a picture of the worst case scenario may not necessarily be a bad thing here, because his friends may not have any idea of the consequences if they have never had any in the past. If your child is an older teenager (14+ for girls,

16+ for boys), be wary not to *tell* him what to do; merely *suggest* things to ensure he doesn't close off and refuse to listen to you. In the end, you need to teach your child how to make his own decisions because you can't do it for him forever. He also has the responsibility to help his friends to do the right thing.

> When our son was about four years old, he spent a day over at his friend's house. His friend was almost a year older than him and was a very boisterous and active child with limited boundaries at that time. After our son came home, he was a little tired, as expected, and he seemed to have had a great time.
>
> Our daughter was only two at the time and was completely in awe of her elder brother. She did everything he wanted to do and really enjoyed sharing playtime with him. She loved cuddling him and we encouraged their mutual affection.
>
> On this day, when our daughter saw that her brother was home again, she happily toddled up to him to give him a cuddle and welcome him back. Her brother's reaction took us all by surprise: instead of reciprocating and returning her cuddle, he pushed her with both hands on her shoulders causing her to fall over backwards, *bang*! Our daughter was so shocked at first – incomprehension taking hold of her – that she paused before finally taking a deep breath and wailing inconsolably – heartbroken.
>
> Our son's behaviour was totally unexpected and totally unacceptable. We immediately jumped into action, picking up our daughter to comfort her, and scolding our son – explaining to him that his behaviour was wrong and to help him see how badly it affected his sister.
>
> Interestingly, our son appeared to be surprised by the reaction to his action. This may have been because he hadn't seen any reaction like this before from us because we hadn't any prior need. But, it may also have been because when he had observed this action before from someone else, there was no follow-up discipline to show whether it was right or wrong, so he thought it was OK to act this way, even though it caused distress to the receiver. Sorry, not on!
>
> In the end, our son was able to recognise that his poor action caused a degree of harm to his sister – only slightly at the physical level (she was wearing a nappy, so her bottom was well-padded), but quite dramatically at the emotional level. We all joined in a group hug – which we did regularly for all sorts of reasons – to finish off the action-reaction process on a positive, forgiving, and loving note.

> Our lesson here was to limit our son's access to his friend, but also to allow for a potential period of disruption and watchfulness upon his return whenever he did interact with him or with other kids too.

Young kids are great little sponges and learn so much just from watching the behaviour of others. That's why it is so important for them to have a role model who is worthy of the task. Also, this occasion taught us that immediate disciplinary action was imperative in arresting a type of behaviour that was unacceptable. If kids get away with it at first, they will try it again. If they continue to get away with it, the behaviour may become a part of their normal interactions with others and that's one reason why bullying behaviour can become entrenched in the playground at schools when largely unsupervised interactions are occurring between kids of all shapes, sizes, and personalities.

It is your responsibility to *do* what you *say*, and *say* what you *do*. When you are consistent with your behaviour towards your kids this provides an environment that is secure, known, and safe. They know what to expect from you because they know your word is your bond. If they do something wrong, then they know they will *cop* it. They will do things to cover up their wrong, but when you discover it, you must discipline them in the same way for that particular deed. This reinforces the idea that every action has its consequences – both good and bad.

The rights of childhood

A child has the *right* to *be* a child.

A child has the *right* to run around and play games.

Every child has the *right* to laugh and to cry.

Each child has the *right* to show all his emotions to the world and not be embarrassed, ashamed or humiliated by them.

Each child has the *right* to make mistakes so he can learn from them.

Every child has the *right* to love and be loved, unconditionally.

Every child has the *right* to become the best person he can possibly be given his talents and education.

The responsibilities of childhood

Please note that as the parent, you need to be able to teach your child what is expected of him. These responsibilities will often be automatically felt and shown by your child, but if any are missing, you need to guide him towards a fuller appreciation of them.

Each child has the *responsibility* to love and respect his parents. This also includes being obedient (when a child) and reasonably considerate (when an adult) to you, especially while he lives with you and while he is under your guardianship, care, and protection. It is his *responsibility* to be as helpful as he can be in his family environment.

Every child has the *responsibility* to be grateful for being alive, no matter who his parents are or where he was born.

Each child has the *responsibility* to be grateful for everything he has been given – small or large.

Every child has the *responsibility* to strive to learn as much as he can during his life.

As your child grows older and becomes a young adult, he also has the *responsibility* to help his friends to do the right thing, especially if they are contemplating breaking the law, or causing harm of some sort either to themselves or to anyone or anything else. This includes dissuading his friends from drug-taking, smoking, and excessive drinking of alcohol. All these things might seem cool and a fun thing to do, but just look at the long-term users and you can see that they usually end up in a very cruel and harmful place. This is not the type of place a true friend would encourage or allow his own mate to enter. It is destructive and unnecessary, and the majority of our society's crimes stem from the misuse and addictive excesses of alcohol and illicit drugs.

Our daughter had been in a relationship with one of the boys from school and she was very attached and devoted to him. After their school time finished and she had gone to university, her boyfriend decided to try drugs. She knew this was bad, but he promised her that it was only for fun. He tried a couple of times to stop using, but it became more than fun and grew into a dependency; he started to deal to finance his growing habit.

His behaviour in other areas was affected and it seemed his entire personality changed and he started to do things that were out of character.

It was a heart-wrenching day when my daughter tearfully called me from his house to ask me to come and pick her up. There were a number of contributing factors to her ending the relationship, one being that he had refused to stop using drugs; he was not the same person with whom she had originally fallen in love.

I was so proud of her. When the realisation of an uncompromising situation finally hits us and we can see it and act upon it, that is a truly great lesson; often painful, but none-the-less great.

If you have a true sense of *responsibility*, you will realise it might not be an easy thing to keep, but it is absolutely necessary to do so.

6

Education or Set a
Good Example

Lead by example as actions speak louder than words.

Instructions:

1. Read the Introduction.
2. Education begins in the home.
3. Teach your child how to adapt to change.
4. Teach your child how to cope with disappointment.
5. Learning should be fun and is best done together.
6. Teach your kids when THEY want to learn.
7. Find the best teaching template for you.
8. Encourage your kids until they succeed.
9. Your kids copy your actions, so do the right thing.

My husband and I share a philosophy of continuing education. In addition to the formal schooling we received and the years at university, we have generally undertaken some form of study or tuition throughout our lives. This has often been relevant to our employment at the time, but not necessarily. It has been both formal, as per a classroom-type setting, and informal, such as being set up in a person's garage. Tuition has included things like oil painting, folk guitar, 2-D animation, basic bookkeeping, and various forms of martial arts, including judo, karate, kick-boxing, aikido, kung fu, and taekwondo.

I encourage you to try any number of pursuits and to stick with the ones that give you the greatest pleasure. Remember that your age is not a barrier to learning, but your attitude may be.

Education begins in the home

Educating your child starts at home. If you are expecting him to learn all life's lessons at school, then that will not happen, so get used to the idea that you are your kid's first teacher. He will learn some social lessons in the playground and, hopefully, academic or technical lessons in the classroom, but his personality is formed and instinctual behaviour is learned in the home environment. By instinctual behaviour, I mean the reactive behaviour that is automatically displayed by a child when he is placed in a particular situation, such as when he initially goes to school, or if he swaps to a new class, or when a new student comes into his class.

In the previous section where discipline was discussed, I related a story highlighting an issue that can arise if discipline is weak or non-existent compared with discipline that is appropriate and consistent. As a parent in the home, you need to ensure your child understands that all actions have consequences. You need to explain those actions that are right and those that are wrong. If he doesn't understand the difference by the time he starts interacting with other kids, he may be in for a rude awakening – and so will you. How many times do we hear stories of parents sending their angel child off to the local crèche, kindergarten or pre-school only to have him return home with every germ under the sun, and also behaviour consistent with some ratbag kid with intravenous red cordial! The change is astounding, and, in many cases, quite unnerving. You need to be prepared for the possibility of it, and have some strategies in mind to deal with what could appear over the next few months. And even if you start with an ideal environment where every child in the establishment is well-behaved and polite, all you need is a new child to arrive who doesn't have the same manners and the whole dynamic of the place can change overnight (or *overday*, as the case may be).

Teach your child how to adapt to change

In other words, how does your child handle *change*? Well, that depends to a large extent on how *you* handle change. For most people, change implies *pain* to a greater or lesser degree and is usually in direct proportion to the amount of *resistance* towards it. The sooner you accept the inevitable change, the less pain there will be. When change occurs, we need to adapt to the new environment.

Forget about wasting energy on trying to maintain the status quo – it's not going to happen – and even if you can change things back to what they once were, it won't last forever and in the longer term, you still have to adapt to some changes. This has occurred through the ages and is the basis of the Theory of Evolution. If we don't adapt, we don't survive.

The same can be said for the microcosm of the family home. For your child to survive, and survive *well* in this world, he needs to learn to adapt to all the changes that will confront him throughout his life, and if he adapts as quickly as possible, he is more likely to benefit than be disadvantaged.

> THE SERENITY PRAYER
> *God grant me*
> *The serenity to accept the things I cannot change,*
> *The courage to change the things I can,*
> *And the wisdom to know the difference.*

Teach your child how to cope with disappointment

Education and learning should ideally go hand-in-hand and be a great experience, but this is not always the case. Many people have fairly bland experiences about their schooling days, some have reasonably happy and fulfilling memories, and others would rather that phase in their lives be completely erased. This may have been because they were severely teased by uncompassionate bullies or by some of the so-called 'cool' kids who believed they were invincible and had the right to pick on anyone they chose, or they may have been too shy, or perhaps just too unaware of what was going on around them.

Whatever your memories of school are, you can improve them for your kids by helping them to cope with the disappointments that come along the way.

If the body is attacked by an infection, the immune system responds almost immediately by sending white blood cells to the site of the infection. This can cause many symptoms that we recognise, such as localised swelling and redness of the skin. These infections will usually be overcome by a healthy and normally functioning immune system, if the infection is not too great. And after our immune system has overcome this infection, it is in a stronger position than it was prior to the infection. It has additional antibodies in its 'toolkit' that it can bring out whenever the same infection appears in the future.

In a similar way, we need to let our kids feel small amounts of disappointment in their lives, so they can understand what it feels like and they realise that they can survive and cope with it. A scraped knee is not going to be life threatening, so when your toddler falls over, give him a moment to reflect on the experience. Let him feel the sensation of pain, and see the skin all scuffed up and (possibly) bleeding. When he has realised that it hurts and starts to cry, then you can comfort him and clean him up. He will be stronger for this accident because he knows exactly what the consequence is of falling over on a gravel path. He will think twice before choosing to run along it next time – that's his lesson.

As your child grows, the disappointments in life will likewise grow in proportion to the experiences he faces. Each experience has the potential to be good or bad, but it should always be a lesson. He needs to learn that life can be good or bad, and that his choices in life – the decisions that he makes – can sometimes fall over (no pun intended). In this case, he has to metaphorically pick himself up, dust himself off, think about what happened and how to avoid it in the future, and start the process all over again.

These qualities of acceptance and perseverance should be fostered from a very early age. If you choose not to allow your child to feel the sting of disappointment as a child, but only a sense of (false) happiness – where mum and dad are doing everything for him and fixing all his little problems and annoyances – he will inevitably be doomed to feel greater disappointment and unhappiness later on as an adult, and what's worse, he won't have any skills in his 'toolkit' to cope with it.

In fact, anecdotal evidence[25] is now showing that more and more young adults in the 20-30 year age group are finding that they feel unfulfilled and unhappy about their lives. Yet they have no apparent reason to feel that way. These people each had a wonderful childhood with totally attuned parents, who helped them all throughout their schooling years – whether in the classroom with maths; or resisting the local bully; or encouraging them to follow their passion and then letting them change it when they discovered they really didn't want to do it; and so on. These young adults had good educations, good jobs, and good relationships – especially with their parents, who were more like their best friends. Additionally, they had nice homes and good health, so why did they feel like they were *empty* or *adrift* and were not as *amazing* a human being as their parent's told them. Why were they indecisive, anxious, and depressed? They had nothing to complain about, so what was the problem?

It appeared that part of the problem stemmed from the parents not allowing their kids to make mistakes and deal with the disappointment that

---

[25] Gottlieb, L. *How to Land Your Kid in Therapy*, The Atlantic Magazine, July/August 2011. http://www.theatlantic.com/magazine/archive/2011/07/how-to-land-your-kid-in-therapy/8555/

usually followed. Instead, these parents jumped in, fixed the problem, and consoled their child with statements like:

That's OK, Johnny. It could have happened to anyone. Don't worry, I'll be able to fix it and it'll be better than ever. If I can't fix it, I'll get you another one.

Looking at these comments as stand-alone statements, they look mainly fine and most people would agree that they will help the child to stay positively focussed and maintain a good self-esteem. But if you take them together as a whole, you will see that they are unrealistically biased towards only a positive outcome.

Those of us who have lived in this life for some period of time (dare I say all who are reading this book) would recognise that there are a whole heap of negative outcomes that occur from time to time, hopefully interspersed with just as many good times. In fact, happiness may be the underlying goal we all crave, but we need to go through many traumas and often quite difficult times to reach that goal. And even when we think we've arrived at it, it seems to dissipate with time. It's a bit like growing up dreaming of marrying Prince Charming, then finding Mr. Right, marrying him, and after a few years, realising he might be Mr Wrong, going through the emotional trauma of separation or even divorce, then realising he was Mr Right in the first place because of all the life-lessons he helped to teach to you.

In addition, by continually praising your child for everything he does, even if the work is mediocre and not particularly good, he may begin to feel he can do no wrong, is always special, and that he is better than others. This type of *helicopter parenting* is misguided as it keeps the *You're Special* belief alive into their child's teens and adulthood. It can come as a horrible let-down when he has to have an ordinary job and drive an ordinary car just like everyone else. The cultivation of this narcissistic attitude in your child is clearly to be avoided. It is a terrible gift to bestow upon one of the most important people in your life.

Keep your feet on the ground, and those of your child. Be supportive and truthful. He must learn about life as it happens, so don't protect him from some of the best lessons he can learn that will allow him to cope with life's challenges.

Learning should be fun and is best done together

Help your kids to love the *concept* of learning. In fact, your kids are born with that concept, so they already have that love. You just need to nurture it and let them blossom to their fullest extent, rather than discourage it by constant criticism and cynical remarks, or smother their innate curiosity by being too attentive and a little over-protective.

Learning should be fun and full of enthusiasm. Sometimes we might not feel particularly enthusiastic about a subject, but if you can dig down to find the main points, expand on them, and then relate them to something that your child knows, this will help your child remember them. If I feel a bit lost sometimes, I just think of the people who are full of enthusiasm and try to emulate them. People like the late Steve Irwin (the well-renowned Crocodile Hunter) or David Attenborough on one of his documentaries. These men are so full of enthusiasm for their subject matter that you can tangibly feel it through the TV screens. If we all had teachers of their calibre and passion, school would be fantastic. Unfortunately, we might possibly be the only teacher for our child who can show those same qualities. This is a big ask for any parent, but your kids are so worth it. If you put the time in to learn with your kids, not only will you all learn something (and not necessarily what you expect), but the process enables you to build immeasurable bonds of love and appreciation with your kids.

OK, at this point I can hear you saying, are you kidding? I don't have enough time to do all the things I should be doing in a day, and now you want me to become my kid's substitute teacher!

Relax! I am only challenging you to do whatever it is you can manage. None of us are superhuman, and neither should we try to be – it's just not possible. Just do whatever is possible, and don't beat yourself up mentally if you can't manage much. At the least, be fully engaged in listening to your child's stories about school and what happened during the day. Listen with attention and make comments that are supportive and encouraging, such as, *Wow, that must have been a bit challenging for you. But, I bet you gave it your best shot, and you should be happy with your efforts as much as your performance.*

Another special time that all parent's should share with their kids is the bedtime story reading. Kids love this and, in anticipation of it, they will usually fully cooperate with the finishing of dinner, cleaning of teeth, and other pre-sleep rituals. Let them choose their favourite book, and every now and again, go out and find a new one. When you read it to them, be as animated as you can; change your voice to relate to the story character, such as make it high pitched if a lady is speaking, or really gruff if it's an old man. Even try different accents. Kids love it and will usually try to negotiate a second reading. A word of caution: if you wish to negotiate additional time, make sure you state the boundary.

OK, I don't mind reading it once more, but you have to promise that you will lie down and close your eyes while I am reading it. Then you have to go to sleep as soon as it's finished.

Make sure they promise to do as you've asked and hold them to it. Otherwise, you might end up with an on-going situation where they will want you to read to them the whole night!

Teach your kids when THEY want to learn

How many times have you heard a story where a child keeps pestering their parent to play with them, but mum or dad is too busy and has other work to do? Then, later on when the parent wants to do something with their child – who now happens to be a teenager – they have absolutely no desire to do anything with the parent and especially are not interested in listening to any advice.

It's a sad story and unfortunately it happens too frequently. As parents, we need to realise that the time to be with and effectively teach our children is when they are most responsive. This time is during their young years – pre-teens – when they are still keen to learn from us and listen to instructions. If the only thing your child learns from you is that rejection is hurtful and that repetitive rejection means he can't learn anything from his parents, then it is no wonder he isn't interested in hearing any words of wisdom from you when he is a teenager.

When a child asks you for information or instruction, then that is the best time to teach him. If you are seriously in a situation where you cannot possibly do anything with your child at that point in time, then make a deal with him to catch up later and stick to it. If you are in business and your best client asks for your help, what do you do? Anything you can to keep him happy. So, treat your kids like your best customers – because they are! And the rewards are so much greater.

When your child asks you a question – and he can ask many, many questions – whether you feel like he is pestering you, is up to you. Isn't it more accurate to say that you are doing something that is too complicated to explain to him, or you don't know how to explain it to him, or you simply just can't be bothered? This is no excuse to become annoyed by him, as his intention is generally not to annoy you (unless he is a teenager, at which time he might have that intention), but to learn from you. So, if you need to put off the learning experience for your child, do it in a gentle and nurturing way so he still feels loved and wanted. Remember, this is your child who will use you as his template for life – warts and all! Wouldn't you like to make sure the template you provide is one of the best?

Find the best teaching template for you

There are a number of ways a parent can try to teach their kids. Depending upon your unique situation, one way or another, or a combination of ways may serve your purposes better. Some are more effective than others and remember that children are great levellers so listen to them and observe their reactions to guide you to your best way.

The first way is the LECTURER type. This has limited effectiveness especially if your child is under the teenage years. His concentration span is usually very small and he needs to be continually stimulated. Expecting a toddler to sit quietly in front of you, while you explain the ins and outs of crossing a road, or riding a bike is just not going to work. After the first half a dozen words, the child will recognise that this isn't for him and start to look around at the walls, ceiling, floor, the dog or cat, or anything else that is vaguely stimulating – commonly called a distraction. When you see this happening, you need to appreciate that you have lost him and unless you change your method immediately, your tiny window of opportunity to get him back will be gone. Clapping your hands, singing a favourite song, or jumping up and down will usually be enough to regain his attention so you can move onto another method with him coming along for the ride. Older kids have usually been through enough of the school system to be able to cope with being lectured. This doesn't mean they like it, or that it is necessarily the best way for them to learn, but they are more used to it.

Another way is the PERFORMER type. This is the parent who shows their kid what to do with or without a suitable explanation and is typically manifested in the parent who is too scared to let their child actually do the activity for themselves. For example, if your child wants to learn how to cut an apple, the PERFORMER will explain the process while cutting it for him, rather than letting him cut it. They are afraid the child will cut his finger. Yet, at some point in the future, the child will want to do it by himself, so he will choose a time when the parent isn't around to stop him. Then the worst fears of the parent may happen if the child hasn't learned the correct technique.

The next, and one of the most effective teaching types, is the SHARER. This parent is actively involved in the teaching of their child using the hands-on method. Simple instructions are explained to the child at each step along the way. The parent shows how to do it the correct way – remember, there may be more than one correct way – and then guides the child to do it after them, allowing the child to touch and feel what is going on. This type of learning experience also allows the child to communicate his ideas about the activity. He may even suggest a way that hasn't been done before, or a more efficient way. Let it happen, encourage his input and be proud of his ideas even if they aren't particularly sensible. He'll improve. Remember, this is a learning process. There aren't too many prodigies in the world, but there are thousands upon thousands of people who never give up until the task has been completed, or the lesson learned.

Encourage your kids until they succeed

Whether you are teaching your child to play with building blocks or ride a bicycle, he can only learn effectively if he experiences it first-hand. If you are the one to teach him, allow him to feel the sting of disappointment when he fails at a task; then help him pick up the pieces and encourage him to have another go until he succeeds. That is a lifetime experience that will be remembered with joy by both of you. It makes the success greater because your child recognises that it didn't come easily, but some real effort was required to complete it. This is an important life skill; to learn persistence until you succeed.

Be aware of what you say to your child and how you say it. If you sound fearful or worried in your voice, you will transmit that feeling to your child and cause him to feel uncertain and off balance. Use phrases like the ones below and say them with enthusiasm, love, and a hint of laughter in your voice:

Have a go at it. I'll watch you and make sure you're OK.
Can you think of another way to do it?
Perhaps you could try doing it this way.

Yes, honey. Sometimes it can hurt when you fall over, but if it's worth doing, then you need to put in some effort to do it. Up you get and have another go.

That's it, you've almost got it!

Keep going, darling. You will get there.

With the right sort of encouragement, kids will make it in the end and really feel like they have been a part of the whole process, not just a bystander. The look of comprehension, understanding, and pure joy on the face of your child when he accomplishes something or learns a new concept is absolutely wonderful and totally rewarding.

Your kids copy your actions, so do the right thing

Did you know your kids are great little copy-cats? Yes, they are. And who do they copy the most? The person who most excites, inspires, and interests them. And during their young formative years and up to their early teens, that means you! But, don't be frightened or flattered. Just be aware that they are watching you when you least expect it or realise it and make sure you are the sort of person who should be copied.

Ask yourself the simple question: *Do I like myself?*

Observe your immediate response. If the answer is, "Not really," then you need to do some work on yourself to improve not only your behaviour, but also your self-esteem.

If your answer is, "Yes, I do," then you have good self-esteem, but not necessarily good behaviour.

You then need to observe the people with whom you mix. If you have nice friends who are good people and valued members of the community, then you are probably a nice person as well. Congratulations!

If your friends have problems (large or small) or issues with the authorities, or, for whatever reason, just don't seem to be able to make ends meet or get ahead in the world, then you are either a very compassionate person who is attracted to trying to help these people, or you could be in denial as well.

The people you attract into your life are the ones you are thinking about the most. For good or bad, you need to ask yourself, "Do I want these people in my life?" These people not only affect you, but they will affect your kids, too. So, make the decision to change if you need to, because your kids lives are now inextricably linked to your own and that of your partner.

Having said that, don't pack up home and move to another country or state just to get away from the people around you. All I'm asking you to do is to think what your best possible outcome could be and focus on that outcome as if it has already happened. Feel the joy of being in that place now and hold that feeling for as long as you can – at least a couple of minutes a day, preferably in the morning before you get out of bed and at night before you go to sleep. This will start a different attraction into your life and you will begin to see the benefits over time. You may start to notice that rowdy neighbours will move away, or the local teenagers find somewhere else to hangout, or you start a conversation with the old couple across the road and you discover they are a wealth of cool information and stories.

With all of your actions, be aware of what you are doing as much as possible. Be an observer of situations, like you're looking at an event that's going on inside a sporting arena. If you are not emotionally attached to the outcome (whatever that may be) then you can be more balanced about the preceding events and hence, act in a balanced way. This is one of the best examples for your kids to emulate.

7

Nice Guy vs Tough Guy

Be a nice guy with good boundaries, rather than a tough guy with hard barriers.

Instructions:

1. Read the Introduction.
2. Set and maintain good boundaries.
3. Discipline your kids from the start.
4. Be consistent with your discipline.
5. Stop bullying before it starts.
6. Teach your kids self-control.
7. When it's over, it's over.
8. Avoid the Blame Game.

You love your kids and you want them to grow up to be the best people they can possibly be with the best opportunities available to them. Every responsible parent wants this same aspiration for their children. Excellent! This is a great gift. This means your kids need to not only have good health and an education, but they need to be able to make friends, too. This means they need to have good self-control and good manners to show respect to other people.

The fashionable media would have us believe that you only need lots of money and good looks to be successful in life, and that the nice guy always loses out and the tough guy gets his way. This is rubbish. There are two perceptions at play here. Boundaries and barriers. Boundaries are a softer approach to conflict and at some point, they may be negotiable, especially with teenagers. Barriers are solid blocks that have no flexibility, nor communication — It's my way or the highway. This tends to encourage bullying behaviour in kids who have grown up this example.

Some parents seem to be confused about discipline and their kids is a choice to be made here.

1. Main point.
2. Have an expansive viewpoint so don't your children feel controlled and in danger that they feel trapped, or
3. Have something in to sweet.

Sounds easy enough, doesn't it. Unfortunately, it is much harder to find the happy medium that most parenting is that is gained through trial and error, education, and experts, well-meaning friends, and family. As previously mentioned, everyone's specific parenting situation is different and this means that what works for one may or may not work for another. Don't let me scare you into paralysis. There are some basic rules to help make your journey through this maze a little easier.

Set and maintain good boundaries

Set your boundaries in concrete. In other words, decide on where your limits of acceptable behaviour lie and then don't budge from them. If someone oversteps those boundaries, then have a strategy already worked out for the consequence. This might be as simple as five minutes in the *naughty corner* for young kids, or grounding your teenager for a week. Make any consequence fair and in proportion with the deed that has been done.

As your kids grow and show more maturity and good sense, some of the boundaries you set will change, become obsolete or new ones will become necessary. An obvious one is bed time – 7:30pm might be bed time for a pre-teen, but a teenager will require more flexibility, especially if he is studying for academic excellence. This doesn't mean you let him off the hook completely. He still needs to get a good night's sleep – which can be up to 10 hours at that age – so he can function properly the next day. In this case, light's out should be around 9:30 or 10:00pm.

Changing boundaries will come gradually if you let it. It depends entirely on each child and their level of maturity. My four kids all had different levels of maturity at different ages even though they had the same boundaries to start. You, as the parent, need to be aware of these differences and make adjustments to suit. If you're not sure, that's fine. Just stick with the old boundaries until it becomes obvious that change is necessary. When it does come, accept it and adapt to it. That's what will help make a big difference in your kid's life and your own.

Discipline your kids from the start

Begin the discipline of your kids while they are young. The younger your kids are, the quicker they learn where the limits are and they will adjust to them. Kids who grow up without limits to behaviour think they can get away with anything. These children will often become the school bully or class clown because they have not learned self-control at a younger age.

Some degree of discipline is necessary throughout life. This is an absolute, so accept this now if you haven't already. If you observe nature in the wild, there is an order to things. Insects are grubs before they pupate and turn into beetles. We don't see a grub saying, "I don't want to waste time as a pupa; I want to be a beetle now!" It just doesn't happen. Animals recognise there is an order in life and they accept it without exception. A pride of lions will kill the weakest animal in a herd and so preserve themselves and the main herd. The strongest survives to reproduce and ensure their genetic material is carried forward into the next generation. Once the lions are fed, they leave the remainder of the herd alone to feed and get on with life. They don't go over to the herd with full bellies and then bully it just for kicks by terrorising the calves and stressing out the parents. It appears that humans are the only animal species on the planet who behaves that way because some individuals mistakenly believe that they have no limits or boundaries to their behaviour.

Be consistent with your discipline

There is a phenomenon in nature called *Cause and Effect*. This is when something occurs (the Cause) to trigger a specific event (the Effect). The same Effect will happen *every* time the Cause occurs. This is called consistency. This is what you must be with your discipline so that your child will quickly learn the principle of Cause and Effect.

If, for example, your toddler pulls your cat's tail (cause), depending on the personality and tolerance of the cat, your toddler will probably finish up with a painful scratch (effect). The same effect will happen every time the cat's tail is pulled. Your toddler will quickly learn that pulling the cat's tail causes pain, so will generally stop doing it. Notice how the cat then continues on with its previous pursuit once its tail has been released. It doesn't hold a grudge against the child and torment it, but it may be a bit more wary of the child the next time they meet.

Stop bullying before it starts

There are two sides to every bullying story:

1. The bully; and
2. The victim.

As mentioned above, the *bully* is often the product of a bad behavioural example learned as a much younger child from someone close to him, but not necessarily a parent. As a young child, he needs understanding and a new environment to help him change his behaviour. As he grows older, he should develop an understanding of what is basically *right* and *wrong* and have the ability to choose the path that is perceptually right for him. This is where a lack of discipline can turn things upside down for these kids.

If he does something *bad* and there are no consequences (discipline), then he knows he can get away with it. If the next time he does it, the same thing happens (nothing), then his perception of the *bad thing* becomes distorted and he sees it as *less bad*. Each time, it is becoming more behaviourally acceptable in his eyes, until it is finally seen as appropriate and normal behaviour. This now affects the way he views the world, and how he fits within it, all the way through to adulthood.

The other side of the story is the *victim*. Everyone pities the victim because he didn't do anything to deserve this treatment – he didn't ask to be picked on! OK, stop here and take a step backwards. If you ask a person who has been victimised what was he thinking or doing just prior to or leading up to the incident, in many cases, he will invariably say that he was worried about being picked on or attacked. BINGO! What has he attracted into his life? What is uppermost in his thoughts? I need help! Yes, he needs help, but not necessarily in the way he expects. He has much more control of his life than he thinks and he can be the force for change himself.

Of course, there are occasions when a victim has been happily going along with his daily activities and then, out of the blue, someone comes along and decides to threaten him. The victim has not been thinking self-destructive thoughts and has not consciously attracted the attack. In these situations, we can't know for sure why it happens, but we can make suggestions. The victim may have had an idea of such a situation imprinted into their mind from a past conversation or observation and, at an unconscious level, the notion has been subtly bubbling along under the surface of conscious thought.

Alternatively, one's own belief systems can also come into play here. Personally, I am a great believer in the Law of Karma: *what you put out comes back to you – good or bad.* The second Law of Thermodynamics basically says the same thing: *every action has an equal and opposite reaction.* So, at some point in the past, a person has done something that is now coming back to them. If you can't remember doing anything that heinous, maybe you are paying back a number of lesser bad deeds that, when combined, have that one weighting.

Whatever the reason a person is victimised, he still needs to get out of *victim-mode* and become self-reliant and confident. How does he do that? By thinking thoughts of self-reliance and self-confidence, then feeling it completely and joyfully, and then visualising a meeting with a bully and having a pleasant experience where he is in control.

If you don't believe me, then imagine you are clapping your hands together, but only using one hand. It doesn't make any noise, does it? In the same way, a bully can only be a successful bully, if there is a willing victim to play the other role. Don't be a victim, be self-controlled.

Teach your kids self-control

There is nothing more attractive in a child than one who has good self-control and self-confidence. In fact, it's a pretty attractive trait in an adult, too.

When my eldest daughter was 13 years old, she asked if she could learn Taekwondo because one of her friends was doing it. I thought that was a great idea and asked my other children if they wanted to learn as well. So we all went along to a class and the kids had a go. They liked it and so I took them along twice a week. My daughter's friend moved away, but the kids still liked it, so we persisted and I joined in after a couple of months sitting on the sidelines thinking, "I can do this."

The great thing about learning a martial art is that it teaches you some life skills – self-defence and self-control – and it also helps you to stay fit and flexible – two of my pet loves. Learning a martial art with your kids also opens up a whole new bonding experience with them – they learn to respect you for giving it a go, and when they see you enjoying it and taking it seriously, they do too. The opportunity for my kids to spar their mother was also irresistible, and vice versa!

We all went through the program for a few years, and my three eldest and I attained our black belts. My youngest stayed for a couple of years, but found she preferred other sports, so she did basketball, dance, and gymnastics instead. There was no issue with this, just a bit of time rearranging to meet our scheduling commitments.

When it's over, it's *over*

After an incident has occurred and you have disciplined your child in an appropriate way, then that is the finish of it. Don't hold a grudge and harp on about the *bad* thing they did, and how you were so *shocked*, and how you *never* want it repeated again...and again...and again.

This only harbours guilt and shame in your child, and also builds up resentment towards yourself. Recognise that we all make mistakes, especially as children because we have so much to learn, and then let it go. As a parent, you will find this harder to do than your child. Kids can recover pretty easily and get on with life, but adults often analyse things and repeat things in their head many times over. If you do this, then I suggest you analyse only to the point of reaching a fruitful conclusion – learn from your mistakes – and then drop it. A good memory in this instance may make you bitter from continual replays of the event and serve no good purpose. Remember, your thoughts become your reality.

Avoid the *Blame Game*

When attempting to solve a disagreement between family members, stick to the facts of the matter and avoid making presumptive judgements. If something valuable in your house has been broken and there are a bunch of kids standing around looking horrified at it, you can be pretty sure that it was an accident. If, however, there is one child who is looking unconcerned and smug, it would not be unreasonable to presume he had something to do with its demise. An interrogation of each child under hot lamps and icy face washers may get you the truth, but usually that sort of drastic action isn't necessary! If your relationship with your own kids is wholesome and open, you only need to ask one of them (usually the eldest) what happened.

You will probably get a number of different versions, or possibly each kid pointing a finger at someone else. If you're still not certain, ask the youngest, as he is often the most open and willing to tell the facts with some minor embellishments (just to make the story sound good).

**When you point the finger at someone else,
remember there are three fingers pointing back at you!**

Nobody will volunteer relevant information if they feel they will be ridiculed or *blamed* for their part in it. Everyone involved needs to be reassured that for a resolution to be found, the truth needs to come out. If it was an accident, then as unfortunate as it is, it wasn't intentional, so whoever caused it needs to sincerely apologise for it, and then the injured party needs to forgive him. If the wrong can be righted, then it needs to be fixed, preferably by the guilty one, unless they are not capable of it.

Each of us tends to have a slightly different view or perspective of a given situation. Our emotional state at the time can *colour* the lenses through which we see things. That's one reason why you may find your kids giving a different account of the same incident. Another reason is that they are simply lying to you.

Why do kids lie to their parents? For the same reason adults lie to each other and the authorities – to point the blame at someone else to avoid punishment. Sometimes, the reason may be more sinister, but unless your kid makes a habit of pulling wings off flies, or setting the neighbour's cat on fire, you are probably pretty safe that you don't have a psychopath in the making living in your house. On the other hand, if your child does like to do these types of things, you should speak with your GP about it and seek some professional help.

According to psychologist Dr. Dorothy Rowe, children start to lie from about three years of age.[26] You can see it happening, especially in someone else's kids. A parent will not necessarily pick up on the subtle lies of their own offspring, particularly if they believe little Johnny is just the perfect angel and wouldn't do such a thing. Or they might just ignore it knowing it is happening at some level, but also not expecting it to be an issue at this stage – after all he's only three!

---

[26]   Rowe, D. *Why We Lie: The Source of Our Disasters*, 2010.

It might be as simple as hearing him tell a friend that something terrible happened, when you know it didn't. This might not mean the child is bad, but merely misinterpreting a situation that is happening around him.

> One mother was telling me that her four year old went up to her kindergarten teacher and said that her aunt was dead!
>
> The teacher was feeling very bad for the family and later in the day spoke with her young pupil's mother, giving her sincere condolences. The mother was quite surprised, but then it was explained to the teacher that the lady wasn't dead, but was in fact a very elderly great aunt in her 90's, who was ill in hospital and not likely to survive the week.
>
> A four year old is not yet capable of working out the intricacies of family relationships beyond a couple of generations, so she made up the gaps according to her current knowledge and logic. She wasn't too far from the mark, but enough to cause some concern, however brief.

Remember that finding someone else on whom you can fix the blame does not solve the problem. It might make you feel slightly better or relieved, but it does nothing else, so move past it. Instead, think about and act upon what needs to be done to set things right.

8

Prevention is Better than Cure

*Avoiding the fall is always better
than mending the broken.*

Instructions:

1. Read the Introduction.
2. Take a First Aid course.
3. Teach your kids how to swim.
4. Stay calm in times of crisis.
5. Maintain a healthy body fat ratio.
6. DNS – Do Not Smoke.
7. DUD – Don't Use Drugs.
8. Reduce the use of anti-bacterial products.

Take a First Aid course

Educate yourself and do a First Aid course. This will give you some excellent skills if something does go wrong and it may also alert you to potential areas within your own home which can be cleaned up or cleared away to reduce the likelihood of an accident.

It's important and you might save a life one day.

Remember that young kids are remarkably fast and a parent only needs to be distracted for just a few minutes for a potential trauma to occur.

Teach your kids how to swim

From the time your kid is a baby, he will usually have an affinity for water. Let's face it, he has been swimming around in amniotic fluid for the past nine months! But, ignorance of potential dangers is just stupidity, so be aware that a baby can drown in just a centimetre or two of water.

The biggest issue I have observed is if the parents – especially the mother – are nervous about water. If you are uneasy about being in and around water, then you could easily pass that insecurity on to your baby. Avoid this at all costs. So, if this is the case, you need to learn to swim as much as your child does. Learn together in a warm and friendly environment and it will further the bonds between you both.

We eventually found an easy way to teach a baby to swim using a full-bodied costume that had upside-down pockets in it in which you could insert foam blocks for buoyancy. There were six pockets and six blocks. So in the beginning, all six blocks were used. They were positioned vertically – three in front and three behind – so this gave the baby room to wave her arms around and kicks her legs without restriction. Her body weight kept her vertical and her head was always outside the water.

We were always in the pool with her and never left her alone. Nothing is worth the risk of drowning. If we had to walk away for any reason, we always picked her up and brought her along with us. A slightly grizzling, dripping child is a far better alternative than the worst case of not having her around anymore. Besides, once she realised she would go back in soon, she calmed down.

After a while, when the baby had developed some ability to tread water and could tolerate the water splashing in her face – blowing bubbles just under the surface of the water is great for encouraging this – we removed one of the foam blocks, starting from the middle back. This kept the front buoyancy the same, but allowed the baby to use her skills more and more.

Over time, another foam block was removed, alternatively from the back and front, and ensuring that the sideways balance was equal. Eventually, they were all removed and the baby could keep herself afloat in the water. This was a great occasion, worthy of a celebration!

It took much more effort and attention to teach our first three babies to swim. But it took about two or three weeks in total to teach our fourth to swim using this method.

Once they have learned to swim, it is such a huge relief!

If you don't know how to swim, go to a reputable swimming school. They will teach you and your baby how to swim. This will give you an amazing feeling of confidence and security, especially every time you go to the beach or visit a friend with a back yard pool.

Being vigilant and watchful is still an important necessity. Children should always be supervised around water. But watching them having fun splashing around is a much better way to spend your time, than constantly telling your child to stay away from the water.

Stay calm in times of crisis

When incidents occur, as they inevitably will, make sure you stay calm so you can assess each situation rationally. Keep things in perspective and focus on resolution, not blame. Here is where your mind control exercises are invaluable. How many times have you, or someone you've known, been present at an accident and either panicked and been unable to assist because they have suddenly transformed into a blithering idiot, or turned into a Nazi ranting and raving about blame and revenge? In either case, the behaviour is not helpful and certainly does nothing towards resolving the current crisis. A better way is to initially minimise any further risk by creating a safe environment. This might be by moving things away from a busy road, or perhaps locking up the dog if it has been involved in some way.

While driving home one time in the early evening, my husband and I got a distress call from our 16 year old daughter, or who we assumed was our daughter, because we couldn't understand a word she was saying through the tears and screaming.

After a number of attempts to calm her down and encourage her to speak slowly and clearly, we finally understood that her pet guinea pigs were at serious risk of being eaten by a snake that had slithered halfway into their cage. We recognized the seriousness of the situation, and suggested all manner of possible actions for her to do that might discourage the snake from going any further, including watering it with a hose – which didn't help, it just moved further inside!

When we arrived home, we found our daughter still very distressed and trying to keep the dogs away from the cage. We saw the snake caught in the wire, but its head was just inside the inner hutch where the animals were cowering.

I lifted the hutch lid to see the guinea pigs were still alive and unharmed, so I grabbed the snake around his middle at the point of insertion into the cage wire and pulled hard. He was a python and not venomous, so I figured if he bit me, I had a good chance of surviving. He started to come loose and as I pulled him free of the wire, I realised that the prospect of coming face-to-face with a very unhappy snake was a pretty high probability.

> I started to rotate with the snake swinging out in front of me (a bit like a lasso) and, apart from one point where I nearly rotated into Frank, I was able to keep the sharp, pointy end away from me quite successfully. We released it towards our grassy hill and it slithered away – if not happily, at least alive.

After you have minimised the potential for more injury, you need to check the injured parties; remember that there may be more than one and just because they aren't bleeding, doesn't necessarily mean that they aren't injured. If people are in pain and obviously suffering, make a quick assessment to determine whether you can handle it, or if you need medical assistance. For example, if your child has tripped over and scraped his knee, there's lots of crying and wailing (sometimes screaming), grabbing of the damaged knee, tears, screwed up eyes, dirt, gravel, cut skin, and a bit of blood. When you stand back (metaphorically) and observe the whole scene, the most important thing for a parent to do in this situation is hug your child.

Give them love and reassurance and say things like:

It's OK, my darling.

You are so brave.

Let me look at it and clean it up for you.

Let me kiss it better.

With this last one, you may be amazed at the healing qualities of a parent's gentle and loving kiss. It comes with a warning though, but it's well worth it. Be prepared to kiss pretty much all wounds that may present to you, whether they are covered in dirt, grit, and blood. You need to learn not to suck in at the same time and only spit out or wipe away the remnants when your child isn't looking up at you with pleading eyes.

> Only one time I didn't do it was when my young son slipped and hurt his groin area and asked for me to kiss it better! I'm not sure if I've traumatised him for life because of my inability to act in this case, but he is currently in a loving relationship with his partner and doesn't appear to be showing any signs of sexual misconduct, or psychopathic behaviour as an adult.
>
> Perhaps if I was more imaginative at the time, I could have *blown him a kiss* by kissing my hand and blowing the kiss towards him and his pained area.

If, however, a hug and a kiss are not enough to calm your child, you need to check for further injuries. Check for broken bones or serious muscle or ligament damage by looking at the injury site and comparing it with the symmetrically opposite part of the body. If it looks pretty much the same, then ask your child to move the injured area. If he can do this easily, then apply some resistance to the movement, such as getting him to wrap the sore finger around yours and asking him to gently pull on it. If he can do this without too much pain, ask him to move the injured part in the four directions – up, down, left, and right – against gentle resistance from you using your hand. If that is still fine, then ask him to put some weight on it, such as standing up on a sore leg.

Each step in the process goes a little further than the last, and it not only indicates to you whether your child is seriously injured, but it shows him a strategy to follow if he is hurt in the future. This is far better than blind fear or panic, and gives him a life skill.

If there are obvious signs of real trauma, such as a bone sticking through the skin in a compound fracture, a visit to the doctor or hospital will be required and as soon as possible.

Sometimes, a child who has been hurt more seriously won't be as noisy as a child who has a little scrape or cut. Also, the sight of blood can be a frightening thing for a young child even if it is the merest speck on the end of his finger. Reassure him, kiss it better, and tell him to suck on it. Unless he has been sticking his fingers in faeces, or other gross things, such as a dead animal carcass, it is reasonably safe to put his fingers in his mouth. Saliva has some antimicrobial properties, and I am more inclined to believe that a child who is gently exposed to the variety of germs that normally exist in our environment has a better immune system because it is always bubbling along underneath hidden away, but still doing its vital role and helping to keep him well.

Maintain a healthy body fat ratio

When I was a kid, nearly everyone was skinny and bony-looking, but there were one or two really fat kids at school who had a *glandular* problem. Their quality of life must have been pretty terrible because they didn't participate in any Physical Education (PE) classes, they looked like they had trouble just breathing, and they were teased mercilessly by some of the less compassionate kids. Also, they must have felt like freaks because everyone would stare at them – obviously or surreptitiously – whenever they would waddle past.

These days, every third kid seems to have a glandular problem. Either we have a highly contagious disease that affects our kids' thyroid glands enough to cause a marked increase in fatty deposits in their bodies, or we have an epidemic of obesity. One of the saddest things, I believe, is seeing these kids from such young ages as two or three years old needing help with tying up their shoe laces for all the wrong reasons. They can't even bend at the waist to see what is happening down there even if they could coordinate their fingers enough to do it themselves. The real tragedy here is the imprinting for their future. They will never know what it feels like to be able to run around all day enjoying playing with their friends without discomfort – climbing, jumping, and running are all fantastic exercises for young kids to participate in because it teaches them balance, coordination, and spatial awareness for the future. These activities use the large muscle groups which help keep the body fit, toned, and healthy. Obese kids can't do these exercises freely and with ease, if at all. Hence, they can't utilise these exercises to lose their excess weight and this may cause them to feel like a failure. Their self-esteem is further assaulted because people will treat them like a freak.

What are we *doing* as parents of these kids? We have to get out of denial, recognise that our beloved child is *actually obese*, and set some boundaries in the home to limit the excesses of food – no fast food, ice cream or pizza for a month or longer. Even if the tantrums come, we have to be stronger because if we don't, then we are condemning our children to a reduced quality and length of life than ourselves. What a legacy to leave your kid? This is misguided love and ignorance of the truth. I know there are some cultural influences that see fat kids and people as healthy or wealthy, but this is a remnant idea from ages long gone, when the class differences were hugely distorted and peasants roamed the streets in rags begging for scraps of food. Malnutrition is still obscenely evident in third-world countries, but the frightening thing in first-world countries is that the incidence is getting higher here as well. It is just hidden under the layers of fat. Fat people – and especially fat kids – are NOT healthy.

Like most things in life, a balance is needed. Falling to one side or the other creates problems unique to the extremes. It's like the pendulum swinging backwards and forwards; being either too fat or too skinny is unhealthy.

Many women strive for the so-called *perfect* body so they can be like a model and have a great image. Unfortunately, this is an illusion because the models who achieve these heights suffer all along the way and have such strict eating regimes that most of us would not be able to maintain them.

In reality, they are undernourished and can have serious health issues over the longer term. Another group who are affected are female athletes who perform strenuous and prolonged long-distance training; they lose their ability to menstruate (amenorrhoea).[27] This may be caused by a number of reasons, one of which is that their body fat is too low. Body fat is one of the easiest components to measure and most gyms can provide this service. It has been suggested that the minimum percentage of body fat that is safe for males is 5% and for females is 12%, though there is little evidence of any benefits for athletes if their body fat drops below 8% for males and 14% for females.[28] For the general population, the typical body fat proportion can vary between 15% and 22%, although it is common knowledge that people within countries adopting a so-called *Western diet* can have body fat proportions at a much higher level.

Within our bodies, the majority of our cells divide and are replaced over time with an average age of all cells in an adult's body estimated to be between 7 to 10 years old, according to Swedish researchers using Carbon-14 dating of DNA within human body cells.[29] Some are replaced within a couple of days, such as stomach cells; skin cells are replaced every 2 – 4 weeks; liver cells are replaced around 300 – 500 days; and skeletal cells are usually closer to 10 years.

A proportion (10%) of our fat cells (adipocytes) are replaced every year, so one could assume that every 10 years, we have a complete set of new fat cells. Interestingly, the *number* of fat cells in adults does not change regardless of an individual's body fat mass or whether they gain or lose weight. This indicates that the number of these cells is set during childhood and adolescence.[30] These cells do not commonly divide and multiply; they merely stretch out and get larger to accommodate the fatty deposits from our food. There are only about two times in a person's life when fat cells do multiply; these are the times when we have a growth spurt as kids. These occur around the age of 30 weeks gestation up to 1 year old and then again between the ages of 9

---

[27] Peterson, L. & Renstrom, P. *Sports Injuries: Their Prevention and Treatment*, 1986; pg 133.

[28] http://sportsmedicine.about.com/od/fitnessevalandassessment/a/Body_Fat_Comp.htm

[29] Frisén, J., Spalding, K.L., Bhardwaj, R.D., Buchholz, B.A. & Druid, H. *Retrospective Birth Dating of Cells in Humans*. Cell Journal, 2005 July; **122**: 133-43.

[30] Spalding, K.L., et al. *Dynamics of fat cell turnover in humans*. Nature, 2008 June; **453**: 783-87.

to 13 years.[31] These are the times when parents need to be extra vigilant with the nutritional needs of their kids. If fatty foods are limited at these times and high quality meals are provided that include fresh fruit, raw or lightly cooked vegetables, lean protein sources, and high fibre grains, then, combined with some regular exercise, the fat cell multiplication will be limited.

It makes sense that the lesser the number of fat cells you have in your body, then the likelihood of you becoming obese later in life is also lessened. Just because a parent is suffering from obesity doesn't necessarily mean that their children will suffer the same fate. Certainly, there could be a genetic propensity which may tilt the scale in one direction, but often if you observe the environment into which the children are placed you can see that diet and exercise – or lack of it – plays a large role as well.

Many obese families are that way because they don't know about good nutrition and they have learned to like nutritionally poor fast food. Also, while they are carrying so much extra weight, the idea of exercise is exhausting and unsupervised activity can often be dangerous. There is no point in having a heart attack during exercise just so you can live longer!

So, go back to the beginning. Eat the correct things from the start and you can avoid so many of the pitfalls of adult life. As a parent, you need to learn to make nutritious meals; they don't have to take forever to prepare either. What could be faster or healthier than a raw carrot – kids love them – or the much maligned celery stick; spread a bit of peanut butter inside it and most kids will devour it.

I have been a vegetarian for most of my life.

As a kid, my mother used to try and feed me meat, but I just abhorred it. A lamb chop would take me about an hour to eat, as I had to cut off every trace of fat before I would put the remaining morsel of meat into my mouth.

I also had to have the meat very well done – almost black – before I would even consider eating it. The blood red of a rare steak, while I understand is mouth watering to some, just makes me want to throw up.

When I was at university, I had to cook for myself, so rice, omelettes, and lightly stir-fried vegetables were my favourites.

---

[31] Salans, L.B., Cushman, S.W. & Weismann, R.E., *Studies of Human Adipose Tissue Adipose Cell Size and Number in Nonobese and Obese Patients.* Journal of Clinical Investigation, 1973 April; **52**(4): 929–41.

Recent research into various degenerative diseases of the body has made me feel so glad that I never wanted to eat meat and that I gave it up entirely while a young adult. Everything from heart disease, various cancers – especially bowel cancer – multiple sclerosis, osteoporosis, and more, have allegedly been attributed to the after-effects of consuming meat – particularly processed meats like salami, bacon, sausages, hot dogs, ham, and other delicatessen meats. Researchers at the Karolinska Institute in Sweden have established a connection between processed meats and stomach cancer.[32] The risk is highest for bacon, so drop that off the shopping list!

Knowing the above, it is also important that you are *happy* when you eat. You need to feel happy about what you eat, when you eat, and why you eat. If you are tucking into a huge T-bone steak or a banana split that is covered in lashings of cream and ice cream and you feel no pangs of guilt (be honest here!), then go for it. But don't do it every day. Give your body the time to recover between these times of excess. As a kid, some foods were considered a treat and we only had them for special occasions like birthdays and Christmas. These foods included ice cream, soft drinks, and lollies. These days, these types of food are available in huge quantities and on a daily basis. Is it any wonder we are becoming an obese nation?

Most of these so-called treats are nutritionally deficient. Think about it. If we actually only consumed the foods our bodies need, then these treats wouldn't get a look in – they are full of sugars (or the more harmful substitute sweeteners, such as aspartame[33]), fats (saturated ones too, which aren't the good fats we actually readily use), and chemicals to make them colourful and tasty. Aspartame reportedly has many harmful side-effects and legal controversy surrounds its release as a food ingredient. I would suggest you research this type of product extremely thoroughly before consuming it. In my opinion, it's not worth the trouble, so just avoid it.

---

[32] www.abc.net.au/health/thepulse/stories/2006/08/10/1710593.htm

[33] Aspartame – an artificial sweetener marketed in products like diet soft drinks and pre-mixed beverages.

ASPARTAME – E951 – NUTRASWEET – AMINOSWEET™

There are over 90 health warnings for this substance including asthma, seizures, memory loss, mood changes, gradual weight gain, headache, dizziness, insomnia, multiple sclerosis, breathing difficulties, depression, and aggression. These adverse reactions can be acute or manifest over time; there is a suspected link to brain tumours; it caused cancer and leukaemia in animal studies; and it is also prohibited in food for infants.[34]

Substances like MSG (monosodium glutamate) are listed on the packaging as Flavour Enhancer 621. This should also be avoided.

MONOSODIUM GLUTAMATE – FLAVOUR ENHANCER 621 – E621

The potential health warnings for this substance include such ailments as heart palpitations, irritability, dizziness, pins and needles in upper limbs, neck pain, bronchospasm in asthmatics, restlessness, headache, heart arrhythmia, migraine, depression, nausea, tingling and numbness; it is prohibited in food for infants. [35]

Perhaps, like cigarette packaging, manufacturers should print out any potential health risks on the labels. Or the health conscious purchaser may refer to books that highlight any potential dangers associated with their use, such as Bill Statham's excellent pocket reference book, *The Chemical Maze Shopping Companion*.[36] The food may look and taste good – and that's really a personal preference as well – but they have a very limited benefit, if at all, and in some cases, they can be harmful.

---

[34] Statham, Bill. *The Chemical Maze Shopping Companion*, 10th Anniversary Edition, 2011, pg 62.

[35] Statham, Bill. *The Chemical Maze Shopping Companion*, 10th Anniversary Edition, 2011, pg 57.

[36] Statham, Bill. *The Chemical Maze Shopping Companion*, 10th Anniversary Edition, 2011. This excellent little book lists the numerical codes for all the approved chemical additives in food and cosmetics in Australian and New Zealand.

It makes me wonder why we spend so much money on health systems when educating the people on the right types of foods can potentially prevent so much disease (by avoiding consumption of toxins) and wastage (due to excessive food spoilage and packaging). We should also develop a social mindset whereby we aren't criticising or judging people who give their kids (just) water to drink, rather than the over-sweetened or carbonated fluids.

DNS – Do Not Smoke

This is a *no brainer.* If you are a smoker, you need to stop. Take whatever steps are necessary to give it up and do it *now.*

Put the money you would have spent each month on purchasing cigarettes into a trust account for your kid. If you spend $400 per month on cigarettes, this is $4,800 per year. By the time your child is 16, you would have saved $76,800. Then, if you add a nominal amount for interest (say, 5% per annum) and have this compounding each year, you end up with a little over $119,000. This is *not* an insignificant amount of money. Any sixteen year old would be ecstatic to receive a trust fund with this amount of money available for him.

Smoking will deny you this dream. Do not put your child through the pain of seeing you suffering in later years. There is no joy here; only short term selfishness, stubbornness, and stupidity; and long term pain, suffering, and anguish. I make no apology about using such harsh words. This cannot be sugar-coated. Ask anyone who has had to watch a loved one shrivel up in front of them, enduring unimaginable agonies, before they eventually die giving final relief and emotional release to those left behind. These are *not* the memories you want to share with your child.

Passive smoking should not be downplayed either. I personally know of two families who had one person in the family being a non-smoker while others within the family smoked heavily. Guess who died first? Exactly, the non-smoker! There are always other factors that come into play, such as stress, obesity, or genetic inheritance, but why put your kids at risk?

Kids who see their parents smoke think it's OK to do it, too. They tend to take it up later on in life, often in their teenage years. This should not happen. It is a total waste and completely unnecessary.

Focus your thoughts on breathing fresh, clean air and seeing you and your kid running around and enjoying a healthy, energetic life. You want to be able to play football, basketball, surf, cycle, or whatever physical activity you choose, with your child throughout his entire youth and teenage years, and beyond.

DUD – Don't Use Drugs

This is another *no brainer*. For a start, it's illegal. So why do something that's against the rules when you're trying to raise your child to be a well-liked and well-balanced member of the community. It doesn't make any sense. If you use it, then it makes you a *dud* in every sense of the word.

Most of us believe that a little use may lead to a larger use, which can lead to dealing and worse. Stop it in its tracks. Don't go down that path and your kids won't be tempted to follow you.

Many people support the idea of using cannabis. There is some evidence for its beneficial use in certain medical conditions, but the risks far outweigh the benefits for the general population. There is a susceptible proportion of people – especially young males with developing brains – who *will* develop a mental illness, like schizophrenia, from using the drug – even if they only use it once.

It's a risk no one should take, especially if it's just to get a temporary good feeling. Why don't you go for a brisk walk, or go on a roller-coaster, or do an aerobics class and wait for the endorphins to flood your body. Our bodies can produce an amazing array of pain relieving and good-feeling chemicals naturally without any destructive side-effects.

Children who are involved in a sport of any kind usually develop good self-esteem and friendships, and are less likely to go down this destructive path.

Reduce the use of anti-bacterial products

You might think I have made a mistake here, but no, I am serious. I feel very irritated every time I see the TV ads for anti-bacterial washes, wipes, and sprays. They send an underlying message that you are not a good housekeeper if you don't use these products. This is a complete lie with a misguided intent. These companies only want to sell their products – they are *not* interested in the health of you or your family.

When I was studying Microbiology, we needed to be very careful about not transferring any pathogens (*bad bugs*) from the laboratory to the outside world. Aseptic techniques were precise and thorough, including the use of an anti-bacterial, anti-viral hand cleaner just before we left the lab. This is entirely appropriate. What isn't appropriate is the assumption that we have such concentrations of pathogenic micro-organisms in our homes.

The average home in the civilised world certainly is covered in micro-organisms, but most of them are fairly benign. If we use products to kill off the standard germs around the home, then this leaves lots of room for the really serious pathogens to flourish because they aren't necessarily killed off by these products and they don't have to compete with the other micro-organisms for living space. These products only ever kill 99.9% of household micro-organisms, and the hardest ones to kill off (the 0.01% left over) can often be the most serious bugs to have lying around.

The solution is fairly simple. Be consistent about the basic cleanliness of your home and maintain good hygienic practices. These include weekly anti-microbial cleaning of your bathroom and toilet, and normal vacuuming and mopping of the floors of your house. Cleaning your bench tops of food and drink spills, and washing your dishes daily will stop food smells taking over your kitchen and living areas. The reason food and scraps start to smell after being left out for a while is because of the proliferation of micro-organisms and their by-products. If you don't create an environment for the germs to flourish, then they won't! So, pack spare food away sensibly and clean up using soapy water and a clean cloth.

The presence of moisture also promotes microbial growth. That's why drying dishes properly before putting them away in cupboards is important. Also, squeeze out as much water as you can from your well-rinsed dish cloth and hang it out to dry overnight to prevent it from smelling and becoming slimy. If it does get all slimy, then wash it or discard it. Don't use it because it will just spread germs wherever you wipe it. The key thing is to have it dry out, as bugs can't grow very well (or at least not in great numbers) without moisture.

Good personal hygiene includes always washing your hands with soap and water before preparing or eating food, and after going to the toilet. Anti-microbial hand washes are not necessary unless you know you will be exposed to the more harmful bugs in larger concentrations.

The more antiseptic our homes become means the less work our body's immune system may need to do. I often wonder if there is a correlation between this and the increase in the number of kids with allergies. How many of these kids were either not breastfed at all or only breastfed for a limited time as babies? And is their home environment antiseptically clean when it perhaps doesn't really need to be?

I know of a family of four: there were two adults and two kids, a girl and a boy.

The father was the breadwinner and dutifully went to work every day. He rarely took sick days, and was content to do the same thing every day.

The mother was the housekeeper and main child-rearer. She worked hard to keep the house immaculately clean – antiseptically clean. In fact, she worked her fingers to the bone scrubbing floors, walls, and benches with methylated spirits. She did not believe a house or room was clean unless it smelled of 'metho'. Her belief system would not allow her to accept that anyone else could clean as well as herself.

Because she worked tirelessly to keep things clean, she was easily upset by someone leaving something dirty lying around. This might be a used plate or glass, but it was also fingerprints and a drop of water on the kitchen sink. As a consequence, she could not accept her children opening the fridge, or helping themselves to any food or drink. She alone was the one who prepared food and put it away.

In spite of their mother's hard work and continual effort to get rid of germs, the children were always sick. In fact, the younger son was a terrible asthmatic from about two years of age. He was also allergic to about 20 or 30 different things. Both the boy and the girl caught every cold or flu that was going around and even with the measles, they both had major complications that were life-threatening. The young son had even gone into hospital at one time under the threat of meningitis, which fortunately, was not the case.

By contrast, the neighbour's kids were always running around outside playing in the dirt. Their noses were constantly running with some form of mucus dripping out of them, so they were not invited in to play with their neighbours.

The 'clean' family tried everything to help their son's asthma – even milk poultices wrapped around his chest at night. Finally, it was suggested to start him on a sport that would keep his lungs active and allow him to dislodge the build-up of mucous, such as swimming or a martial art. They tried this and it worked. After a number of years, his asthma became less life-threatening and more controllable.

Additionally, when he went to university, he was able to undergo weekly allergy injections. The theory of these injections was to gradually increase his exposure to the allergens and help him to build up a tolerance over time. After a number of years, he was able to tolerate most of them and remained intolerant to only about half a dozen potential allergens.

The question we have to ask here is did his own mother unknowingly put him at more risk by keeping the environment in which he lived almost sterile? Certainly, there are many factors involved here, including genetics, but knowing that at least 50% of the ancestral gene pool was sourced from a line of nonagenarians, one wonders whether a strategy of gentle introduction to environmental allergens as the boy was growing up might have enabled him to avoid the host of allergies from which he suffered.

When you have kids, you have to make a choice about whether to keep your house so sterile that it loses its value as a *home* and merely becomes a *dwelling*. Life doesn't have to be that hard.

9

Parents and Friends

A parent's job is to provide a safe place for their kids.

Instructions:

1. Read the Introduction.
2. Be a parent first and a friend later.
3. Let your kids develop at their pace.
4. Discourage underage drinking.
5. Let your kids choose their own friends.
6. Respectful communication needs to be both ways.

Parents need to participate in their kid's life as guides and mentors, and not just spend lots of money on him in some sort of attempt to make him happy, while ignoring their main role as his carer.

Be a parent first and a friend later

It seems that some parents get a little confused about whether they should be their kid's friend as well as their parent. It's really quite simple.

You need to be a parent first with all the duty of care and responsibility that this position holds, even if it means that you might not be liked once in a while. As emotionally painful as it may be at the time for both of you, your child will benefit from a parent with a strong purpose and value system. Consistency and mutual respect are the key elements. Lose these and you will have some troubled times ahead. This doesn't mean you can't have fun with your kids – quite the opposite. The time spent between parents and their kids should be fun and enjoyable; that's the whole point of it. It just needs balance.

After your child has grown up enough to have developed a good sense of right and wrong so he can make more of his own choices in life, you can step back a bit and be more of a friend to him.

Be aware that even when your child has become an adult there will be times when you are still needed as a parent. Often, these may be in times of great stress or grief and all you can do is be there with a loving hug, a kind word, or total silence, and that is all that is required.

A parent's job is to provide a safe place for their kids and that continues on for a lifetime.

Let your kids develop at their pace

Each of us develops in such a way that is unique to ourselves. Your parents did it, you did it, and your kids will do it. If we try to fiddle with this process, either by speeding it up or slowing it down, we can cause harm to our child and the environment in which he lives.

SCENARIO ONE – SPEEDING UP THE GROWTH PROCESS

Close your eyes and imagine you are sitting in an audience of parents and kids waiting for a set of stage curtains to open. The MC steps out, introduces herself, then proceeds to introduce a pretty young girl who is covered in make-up and bling. Her dress is an explosion of frills, satin, and lace in an attempt to display her as the starlet she 'wants' to be. She has talent; she can sing in tune; tap dance; do cartwheels, spins, and splits. She is only five years old. She finishes and everyone applauds. The MC introduces the next little girl; just as pretty, talented, and gaudy. After the tenth child comes out, you start to wonder if someone is producing clones behind the curtain.

Finally, it ends, and the winner is announced. The girl is ecstatic and cries she is so happy. All the other girls cry because they didn't win. And then you see the mothers! A shudder passes down your spine as you watch these ladies – many of them obese, and all, like their daughters, wearing too much make-up. The winning mother rushes up to her daughter with wild shrieks of joy; practically deafening those around her, and knocking over bystanders in her haste. Meanwhile, all the other mothers are attending to their charges with differing approaches. Some are consoling their daughters with kind words and hope for better luck next time; others are angry and accuse the judges of bias; while still others are envious of the winner and hope some terrible ailment will befall her.

This type of scenario works the same for the obsessive father who wants his son to be the star sportsman and forcefully directs him along this path in spite of physical injury and emotional trauma.

Not only is there a terrible example being set for these kids, but they are still so young that they can be easily manipulated by the people around them. Yes, the mothers will swear on an oath that their daughters *want* to do these pageants, but what started them there in the first place? It's because of an influence that has come from the home environment, more than any other place.

So, watch your behaviour to make sure you don't do things inadvertently to set your kids on a treadmill from which they might not know how to get off gracefully. If you want to do something in your life, then do it yourself or step back gracefully if your time to achieve it has passed. Don't live off the reflected glory of your kids. Let them have their own dreams and ambitions; and let them do it in their own time.

Scenario Two – Slowing Down the Growth Process

Picture a child of about two years of age. He has just fallen over. Before he starts to cry, in fact, even before he feels any pain, his mother picks him up and smothers him in kisses and hugs and entirely distracts him from the accident. She hands him a lolly pop to ease his pain.

Now see this child at about four years old; just starting pre-school. The child is clinging to his mother's leg and won't let go. He screams and squeals and all the other kids are staring at him. A couple of them start to look worried and begin to whimper themselves: *Is this school thing a good idea? He doesn't think so; maybe it's scary?* Other mothers are glaring at the screaming child's mother and muttering under their breath. In the end, the mother gives in to the child and carries him back to the car and takes him home.

The boy is now 13. He is badly over-weight, weak-spirited, and generally unliked by his class mates. He bears the brunt of the local bully's teasing and is often absent from school. He has poor health and his obesity denies him a chance to participate in sports, so his school life is pretty sad and lonely.

He has survived his teens and twenties and is now 36, is on a disability pension and still lives at home with his mother. His father died when he was 15 after which time he disappeared into his shell completely. The son spends most of his time on the internet, playing fantasy and war games, and communicating with other people from around the globe. He has re-invented himself as a man of great skill and ambition, but it is only in his imagination. The real world is painful and dark to him. He feels like a stranger in it, yet his fantasy world (online) allows him to excel and achieve great things.

> This man's mother is still looking after him. She provides him with three meals a day, washes his clothes, and cleans up after him. He has few life skills and can barely look after himself.

What will happen to this man after his mother dies? She has helped to create a very unskilled person who is content to live off the hard work of others. I'm sure she didn't mean to do this, but her misguided efforts under the guise of *love* have almost completely inhibited his emotional growth. If she had let him fight some of his own battles as a child, he would have grown stronger and more confident in his own abilities.

Let your child grow up naturally and explore the world around him. With parental encouragement and support, he can be confident in the choices he makes. The more practice he gets making decisions as a child will allow him to find the task easier and more natural as an adult.

> The *mistakes* that we make have the potential to teach us great *lessons*, so look at all *challenges* as learning *opportunities*.

Step back a bit and resist the urge to *direct* your child on a career path; forcing him to do what *you* want him to do. Instead support his preferences and let him find out whether they are worthwhile. Introduce your child to a wide range of careers; everything from the traditional to the more adventurous types, such as the military, sky-scraper window washer, or park ranger. There are so many from which to choose; they are being invented and re-invented all the time. Some kids change their mind like the wind, so don't panic if he chooses something a bit risky at first, such as a sky-diving instructor. However, if he really wants to do that, it will become very clear in the ensuing years whether his passion and interest in life is heading down that path.

> When my brother was a little over two years old, my mother was preparing to have her third child. My sister was only 16 months old when I was born.
>
> Years later, when researching some information for a book about my mother, one of her old friends was telling me about when she used to babysit my siblings. My brother would only relax and calm down if she got the vacuum cleaner out for him to play with, and my sister always had a fascination for mum's rings, so she would carry them around in her apron pocket.

> My brother's interest in the way things worked, and my sister's in the way things looked, motivated them to choose a path that would provide them with those special things in life.
>
> My brother studied and topped his year in aeronautical engineering and has a light aircraft pilot's licence, while my sister became a dentist, specialising in periodontics (gum diseases) and she has many beautiful things, including rings.

If we help our children develop their interests and skills to the best of their ability, that's doing a great job as a parent.

But, I hear some of you ask, what if my kid has no idea what he wants to do? That's fine and quite normal. Many of us don't really know where we are going to end up, so while we are young, it's good to get out there; try lots of different things and see lots of different places. It's a bit like a smorgasbord; the more choices you have, the better your choice will be in the end. And if you don't like your first choice, you have plenty more from which to choose.

> Two of my kids didn't have a set goal in mind, so they weren't particularly interested in school from an academic point of view. However, they still finished their Year 12 and made some great friends. One finished a qualification in Hospitality, but after a year decided it wasn't really for him. He loved martial arts, and instead, decided to study Kung Fu. He was passionate about it and practiced it six days a week. A year later, he won regional, state, and national awards for one of the forms or kata of the discipline. He performed it brilliantly. He has since formed a loving relationship with his partner; briefly joined the Army; been in his own small business and with that experience behind him, is looking to work in the mining towns for a couple of years.
>
> My daughter decided late in her Year 12 that she wanted to do Psychology. She picked up her studies, and did well enough to get into that course at university. But her passion waned and she deferred for a couple of years, eventually dropping it entirely. She has been working in the retail sector since then, and is making noises about returning to study and university, but she isn't sure what she wants to do. So we patiently wait.
>
> The other two kids were more focussed: one wanting Army life and the other to be a Veterinarian.
>
> One was advised to complete his Year 12, which he did and because of the lack of pressure, he passed it very well, and really enjoyed it. One of his

favourite subjects was Physics, but also Technical Studies, which is another name for Wood and Metal work. He made some great things: really beautiful and functional. He also kept himself physically fit and was a member of a school team to complete the gruelling Kokoda Challenge on the Gold Coast hinterland. The course runs up and down hills and valleys for 96km and the cut off time is 33 hours. His team completed it in 30 hrs. It was an amazing accomplishment. My dad (who had been deployed to New Guinea during WWII) was there to see him cross the line and win his own special 'dog tags'. It was a very proud moment for us.

When he joined the Australian Army, it was an emotionally charged occasion. But, apart from a couple of challenging weeks during the initial recruitment training, he has thrived and flourished. His further growth and maturity occurred during his deployment to Afghanistan, where he soon learned about different cultures and peoples. The day he came home was very special. He proudly showed us his 'gongs' (medals) and was slightly amused that he could now be referred to as a 'veteran'. He is looking forward to his first Anzac Day as a 'vet'.

Our youngest child has always had a love and affinity for animals; willing to take in every possum or tawny frogmouth that is lying by the side of the road. She has talked us into many pets, and I guess because her parents are both softies in that area, we are prepared to accept them. So having a passion like that leans pretty heavily towards Veterinary Science. She studied very hard for her Years 11 and 12, and resulted in a very high score (equivalent to around the 92nd percentile). Unfortunately, she didn't make it into Vet Science even with that score, but her second preference was Biomedical Science. The first year of this course does about 80% of the same subjects as first year Vet Sci, so we are all hoping she can be accepted into the course in the next year.

Then maybe we will have two 'vets' in the family.

Discourage underage drinking

One other topic I would like to touch upon is *underage drinking*. Some people actually believe that there is nothing wrong with giving their children alcohol to drink at a young age. How can I put it: WRONG! Alcohol kills off brain cells, so maybe that is why these parents think it is OK to give to kids.

It's not. It destroys a young person's brain cells just as much and can set them on a habit that is so destructive to a normal and balanced life.

In many cultures, there is a very open and relaxed attitude about allowing young people to drink. In these situations, you need to look at what is actually happening. It is part of a ritual where everyone shares all the food, wine, and entertainment that is being offered. In the environment of a happy family gathering with copious quantities of nutritious foods; laughter and merriment, there does not appear to be any long term harm. The emphasis here is not on the alcohol, but on the food and the enjoyment of the occasion as a whole. The child is eating lots of food which helps to absorb and dilute some of the destructive effects associated with the alcohol that is being consumed, but the brain cells are still being affected; just to a lesser extent. That is an undeniable consequence.

More disturbingly is the growing culture of *binge drinking* among young people. The focus is *only* on the alcohol and how soon they can make themselves completely paralytic. They are doing themselves serious harm, not only physically, through accidental injuries, but emotionally and mentally as well. Parents should be actively discouraging this type of behaviour, not condoning or ignoring it.

Schoolies is a rite of passage undertaken at the end of Year 12. It occurs in a number of locations around the country, but its locus is usually Surfers Paradise on the Gold Coast and during that week, the city is inundated with around 120,000 kids aged 17 or 18. The legal age for drinking alcohol is 18, so there is an extremely high risk of underage drinking in this environment.

As a parent, there are always concerns in allowing your kids to attend such an event. The best you can do is to educate them on the potential risks of having their drinks spiked, unprotected sex, assault by *toolies* (older predators), drug use, and drunken brawls.

If you trust your kids and encourage them to always stay in a group of their friends and to look out for each other, then that puts the onus back on them, and for the majority of kids, they are worthy of that trust. Thankfully, my kids all had a pretty benign experience with Schoolies.

What disturbs me more is the fact that many parents buy the alcohol for their underage kids and take it up to their hotel rooms in eskys. This is just wrong! It is encouraging the worst type of behaviour – that of dishonesty and stupidity.

Let your kids choose their own friends

As part of the growing up process and instilling trust and confidence into your child, you need to allow him to choose his friends. This is one area where parent's should sit back and observe. If your child makes a mistake with their choice of friend, it will soon become apparent, and if you have been a good role model, they will recognise this and part from them without much (if any) intervention on your part.

When one of our sons was about 13, one of his school acquaintances visited our home. He managed to get into a scuffle with another boy who was visiting our daughter. They pushed a door handle through the wall and then they both promptly took off.

After speaking with my father about the incident, he came with some tools, materials, and colour-matched paint to fix the hole and showed his granddaughter what to do. She did a brilliant job of fixing the wall; it looked like new. I was very impressed by her efforts.

The corollary to the story was that our son completely withdrew any friendship he may have felt for this other boy; in fact he regarded him as a complete moron after that, and neither boy ever graced our doorstep again.

As parents, we didn't have to say anything. Our kids already knew which behaviour was appropriate and made their own decisions regarding this matter.

Sometimes a situation may arise when one of your child's friends feels that they should compete with you for your child's attention. This is an obvious power play and usually starts when the friend doesn't feel they can control your child enough for their purposes. Now, these purposes may be pretty harmless – especially when the age of the friend and your child is quite young – but they can have more sinister undertones if the friend is many years older than your child, or if your child is well into their teens.

This situation may arise if there has been a period of non-communication between yourselves, as parents, and your child. When this happens, your child may have lost some degree of respect and trust in you and this void in their lives could be filled by someone else. This may leave your child vulnerable to potentially unscrupulous characters, so it should definitely be avoided.

Respectful communication needs to be both ways

As a parent, you need to be behaviourally consistent. This requires great strength of character, but is so worth the trouble. I don't mean standing at the front door with a baseball bat waiting for your kids to come home, but always showing them your love for them, that you trust them, and by reacting to similar situations in the same way. You, as the adult, need to show the correct behaviour and always be the first to end a dispute if a stalemate has been reached. Start talking calmly and clearly, without blaming anyone or making a judgement about either your child or their friend. Structure your questions in such a way as to avoid the appearance of an interrogation session. Begin the discussion with the steps leading up to how you (as the parent) are feeling now. This provides a period of time for your child to gain more of an understanding of where you're coming from, and also gives him an opportunity to gather his thoughts for when he should answer. Use open-ended questions, such as those beginning with why, where, and how. Your child cannot just answer with a *Yes* or *No*, even though sometimes that's more informative than the often used *Humph*.

If you can get nothing more than a few grunts out of your child, stay calm and focussed and say things like:

I know you're not ready to talk about it right now, so we can do that whenever you're ready. Just give me some notice in case I have to leave work, or postpone someone or something else. It really does matter to me to know you're OK, so I'm always happy to make time for you.

This leaves the door open to work out a solution at another time. It tells your child that they are more important to you than anything else and that you're not angry with them. When fear is taken out of a situation, then good communication can occur because no one is scared of the consequences of what might be discussed. This also suggests to your child that they should respect your prior commitments and not expect you to do unreasonable things for them.

10

Baby Basics

They are their own perfect person.

Instructions:

1. Read the Introduction.
2. Delight in your baby's perfection.
3. Keep your baby warm and secure.
4. Change nappies ASAP.
5. Feed your baby.
6. Clean your baby's teeth.
7. Bath your baby.
8. Exercise with your baby.
9. Socialise with your baby.
10. Travel with your baby.
11. Putting baby to bed.
12. Actively picture and feel the best outcome.
13. Avoid guilt trips.

Delight in your baby's perfection

After a child is born, everyone checks for the basics, such as gender, ten fingers, ten toes, two eyes, two ears, a nose, and a mouth. If there is something different at this stage, other forces come into play, such as paediatricians and other specialist doctors. Children with special needs may be physically different, but not necessarily different in other ways, and they need just as much love and understanding as a normal kid. By the way, there is no such thing as *normal*; statistically speaking, a normal child is just one who is significantly similar to other children, or in other words, is in the majority group.

The new parent becomes immediately aware of the larger and more obvious systems of the skeletal (bones), muscular (fleshy bits), respiratory (wailing cry), digestive (feeding and pooing) and urinary (weeing) systems.

We notice how our new baby is incredibly flexible. Every bone, muscle and joint is perfect and can be moved around to the fullest extent for its specific purpose. There are no injuries, fatty deposits or arthritic issues troubling this pristine body. We stand in awe of the perfection before us and hope it will always be like that for him, and comparing ourselves, wonder how we came to be so limited. He epitomises how the musculo-skeletal system should work.

Watching the rise and fall of your sleeping baby's chest can be so calming and reassuring. We see that this perfect little being is already independent – his own body is functioning to make him breathe all by himself. You don't have to do anything for this to happen. Certainly, we need to be there to nurture him to maturity; to feed and burp him; to wash and clean him; to love and guide him; but your baby is already his own person. His journey has commenced and you can participate with love or with fear – the choice is up to you.

Keep your baby warm and secure

The *ah-waaa* cry of a new-born baby is quite recognisable and heart-wrenching. The natural response is to pick up the baby and cuddle him. And this is exactly what you should do. New-borns have been so used to the restricted movement, muted sounds, warmth, and cramped quarters of the mothers who carried them for nine months, that when they are left alone, or feel hungry, cold or exposed, they immediately feel insecure, unhappy, and may start to cry. Wrap your baby up securely and cuddle him calmly until he has relaxed and fallen asleep. If he doesn't settle straight away, then you need to check the basics: dirty nappy, too cold, too hot or hungry.

Change nappies ASAP

Changing the baby is definitely an experience to be shared by both partners because a dirty nappy should be changed *as soon as possible* after the event has occurred. Baby's skin is very soft and delicate and the acidic content of wee (urine) can be quite burning to it. The first poo (meconium) from your new-born baby can be quite a shock. It consists of bile, intestinal debris, and mucus, and can leave you wondering whether the smell has come from your baby or some unseen extraterrestrial! Remember that baby has been ingesting all sorts of things that have been floating around with him while in the womb.

> **TIP: Breathe through your mouth when changing nappies. This makes it possible to do the job without being overcome by the smell and being sick yourself.**

While your baby is feeding exclusively on milk, his wee and poo will be relatively benign, though still capable of causing angry rashes that are painful. Once he starts on solids, then his faeces and urine will be stronger as it contains remnants of gastric juices (acid), microbial waste, undigested food, and uric acid (more acid).

> My child developed a nasty rash on his bottom, so I tried everything to remove it: creams, powders, waterproof rubs, and open air – you name it, I tried it.
>
> A friend's father (who was a doctor) suggested I try using disposable nappies for a while. I had always felt disposables were a waste of money and bad for the environment, but I was desperate, so I tried them. After a few days the rash subsided and stayed away. This gave me the opportunity to get back to a baseline with my baby and be more fastidious with the barrier creams. I went back to using cloth nappies, but always kept a few disposables around, just in case.

When you change your baby's nappy remember to respect your back. You will be doing this job for years, so make sure you have a proper change table with a bench that is a little higher than your waist height. This will stop you bending over too much. There are some well-designed tables that allow you to have everything you need within reach, or you could just set your table near a wall with some handy shelves on it.

The basics you need are:

1. A soft under cloth on which to place the baby and to soak up any leaks. Use any spare cloth nappies, old towels, or bunny rugs. Baby needs to be lying on his back (supine). If your baby is very young, support his head with one hand.
2. A bin (with lid) in which to place dirty nappies.
3. A few soft cloths to wipe baby clean. This could be a set of clean face washers which have been bought specifically for this role – plain white is best. Dampen them with warm water immediately before using them. After washing and thoroughly rinsing, hang them up in the sun for some UV sterilisation and bleaching. You may also prefer to use disposable wipes, though these are less environmentally responsible, but can save you time.

The trick with boys is to always leave a cloth on top of their groin area just in case they sprinkle you with their little fountains (keep your mouth closed, too!). If your baby boy has not been circumcised, you will need to gently wipe away any muck that may have collected there.

With girls, you need to always wipe from their front to their back so their vagina stays clear and clean of any faecal matter. There is a thin layer of skin covering the opening of the vagina (hymen) which should be intact and hence prevent too much muck getting stuck down there.

4. A gentle tickle and blurt with your mouth on your baby's clean tummy. This makes the whole experience fun and a big giggle.

5. A good barrier cream to rub all over the skin that will be enclosed within the nappy.

6. Plenty of clean, fresh nappies. Place one under your baby's bottom and secure it to fit snugly. If you use a cloth nappy, make sure all the cloth is tucked into the plastic panty that fits over the top. If it isn't, then baby's clothes will get wet next time he does a wee (No. 1). Be aware that baby's faecal discharges (No. 2) are very moist at this time, so they can run up baby's back and appear where you don't expect them to be (sometimes referred to as a No.3!).

7. If necessary, have a new set of clothes available for baby to wear, just in case the previous ones were soiled.

Feed your baby

The preferred method for feeding your baby is to breastfeed. If you can, exclusively breastfeed your baby for the first six (6) to twelve (12) months of age as this will help set baby up for life. The breastfeeding timeframe varies greatly between different mothers and babies, so do the best you can because the longer you can breastfeed, the better it is for your child.

I was fortunate to be able to breastfeed my firstborn for just on six months. With each subsequent baby, I was able to increase that timeframe by about another month, so that when my fourth child came along, I was able to breastfeed her for ten months.

Breastfeeding benefits both the baby and the mother:

1. Breast milk is species-specific – it is tailor made for human babies and contains the perfect balance of nutrients at this time.
2. Breast milk is usually ready to go 24/7.
3. Breast milk contains antibodies (immunoglobulins) to help your baby stay healthy by fighting off infections and allergies.[37] A baby's immune system can take between two to six years to fully mature, so it needs all the help it can get.[38]
4. Breastfeeding your baby will help the mother's body to return to its normal pre-pregnancy state.

If you are concerned about whether breastfeeding will affect your breast shape for the future, don't be. I had a *D* cup prior to my babies arriving; this went to about an *EE* during the breastfeeding time period; and it actually dropped back to a *C* during the subsequent years. Since then, it has gradually returned to a *D* size.

I believe having a correctly fitting and supportive bra from the onset of puberty makes more of a difference. My preference is to wear a sports bra because they are the most supportive and comfortable.

Also, when you exercise, remember your upper body and arms. Swing your arms when you walk and do push ups, too. Start with pushing off a wall, then over time, gradually step further away from the wall as your arm muscles develop and can support your weight better. I can only do push-ups from the floor on my knees because full ones aggravate an old shoulder injury. Just do what you can and saggy boobs shouldn't be a part of your future image.

Whatever you decide, please don't use breast shape or size as an excuse *NOT* to breastfeed your baby.

When your baby is hungry, you should feed him when he starts to show hunger signs, such as more agitated movements; sucking on his fist or object placed near his mouth; turning his head toward you with mouth open if you

---

[37] Xanthou, M. *Immune protection of human milk*. Biology of the Neonate. 1998 Aug;**74**(2): 121-33
[38] Goldman, AS. *The immune system of human milk antimicrobial, antiinflammatory and immunomodulating properties*. Pediatrics Infectious Disease Journal, 1993 Aug;**12**(8): 664-71

hold him in the feeding position – head in the crook of your elbow while his body lies horizontally across your body – or, as a last resort, crying. The important point is to place the entire nipple – including the darker coloured areola surrounding the nipple – into his mouth. This is the only way he can really latch onto the breast and begin sucking effectively using his tongue and upper palate of his mouth.

Breastfeeding can also help the mother keep her own breasts healthy, by reducing the risk of cancer later in life,[39] and it encourages the uterus to shrink to its normal pre-pregnancy size. The initial sucking from the baby triggers a *let-down* reaction, where the flow of milk increases dramatically. This was another wonderful feeling and again I would sit in awe as I observed my body do another amazing thing without my conscious thoughts causing it to happen. At this time, the other breast would often leak, so pads were very useful to use on it. Using both breasts at each feed is preferable because it can help keep the ducts free of blockages. Alternating the starting breast can also help minimise problems because the let-down reflex can then occur with a different breast each time. It's a good idea to tie a piece of ribbon or safety pin to your bra on the side you need to start with next time and just swap it over every feed.

Mastitis is a painful inflammation of the breast that appears as a red area on the skin of the affected breast. This usually occurs if a duct has become blocked and infected. Sometimes a dose of antibiotics is necessary to clear the infection, but often it can be treated by massage, expressing the excess milk from the breast, or by encouraging the baby to feed from that breast first time for each feed until it clears up.

It is preferable to feed your baby when he wants it for a number of reasons:

1. Like us, your baby knows when he is hungry. Denying him food can cause undue stress to both the baby and the parent, and can sometimes delay attachment to the nipple until he calms down.
2. If the mother has a smaller capacity to store breast milk it will be necessary to feed more frequently than a mother with a larger capacity for storage.

---

[39] http://www.nytimes.com/2009/08/11/health/research/11cancer.html

---

More on Capacity to Store Milk

Research has shown that the maximum amount stored by one mother was 300% more than the maximum amount stored by another mother.[40] So, this mother was able to provide her baby with three times the amount of milk in one feed, than the other mother, who needed to feed her baby three times to give the same amount of milk. However, over a 24 hour period, both mothers had the ability to produce the same amount of milk. So the number of feeds you may need to give your baby over a 24 hour period may depend on your body's ability to store milk over that time.

My first child took three months to begin sleeping through the night. It was in the middle of winter and I used to get up to feed him in a chair and do everything that I was told I should be doing.

My life was in limbo.

Every day rolled into the next and I felt like I was an automaton that could only perform those tasks that had to be done – feeding the baby, changing the baby, bathing the baby, and washing nappies. Anything extra was either impossible or an absolute necessity, such as personal meals and hygiene.

Shopping? Hah! Now that was a real event! It felt like I was moving house every time I had to take the baby somewhere – nappy bag, pram, spare clothes, vomit cloths, lotions, bottles, practically everything but the kitchen sink.

It took me three months before I could even begin to feel vaguely alive or awake and this correlated directly with the amount of sleep I had managed to glean the previous night. I had just had four hours straight sleep – what a miracle! I could relate to why sleep deprivation was such an amazing torture technique. Waking up every 30 minutes would bring me to the point of vomiting, but that little wailing machine in the next room just kept on and on relentlessly.

My second baby was an absolute dream.

She started sleeping through after one week. She was also a winter baby, but instead of getting up and freezing every time a night feed was due, I did the unthinkable and fed her in my bed. We had been warned *NOT* to feed the baby in bed for fear of crushing or smothering the newborn.

---

[40]   Daly, S. and Hartmann, P. *Infant Demand and Milk Supply – Part 1 Infant Demand and Milk Production in Lactating Women.* Journal of Human Lactation I 1995; 1: 21-26.

My experience of this was completely different – maybe because I am a small framed person, I can't be sure.

Not only did we both stay warm and comfortable, but I was more relaxed and able to breastfeed more effectively. Even if I drifted off to sleep, I was not able to fall into a deep sleep. Every little noise or movement from the baby stirred me awake. I was cognizant of her presence the whole time.

I kept her bassinet next to my bed, and when she had fallen asleep, I simply put her back into it.

It was so easy by comparison with the first time.

One conclusion that could be drawn from this experience is that as a first time mother, my body – both physically and emotionally – had not yet completely understood what it was supposed to do, and I was not able to coordinate the production of enough milk. However, the second time around, my body remembered what it had to do and could produce and store enough milk by the second week to allow my baby to be fully fed in a much earlier timeframe.

Interestingly, the capacity to store breast milk is not related to the size of the mother's breasts, so a mother with large breasts may not necessarily be able to store more milk than a mother with smaller ones.

Western culture is one of the few where people do not co-sleep with their babies. If you're a smoker or drinker, I would definitely not sleep with a baby. But if you're not, then try it, making sure you put your arm at a right angle (90°) on the side where baby is sleeping to ensure you can't roll onto him.

3. The timing interval and length of a feed may differ according to what is being fed to the baby: breast milk, bottle fed with breast milk, or bottle fed with formula milk.

Breast milk

The composition of breast milk varies at the onset of breastfeeding and during individual sessions. In the first few days after the baby's birth, colostrum[41] is released and thereafter milk is produced, which includes foremilk containing non-fatty components. It is important

---

[41] Colostrum – nutrient and antibody-rich yellowish fluid

to completely empty each breast as your baby feeds because this helps to stimulate the production of more milk for next time.

In addition, studies have shown that the concentration of milk fat increases with the length of the feed.[42] Milk fat helps determine the caloric content of breast milk and this may be used to indicate the *quality* of the milk in terms of satisfaction of hunger. If baby falls asleep before completely emptying the second breast, just start the next feed with this breast, or you could use a breast pump to fully empty the breast and hence have a supply waiting in the fridge for baby in case you need it.

MORE ON IMMUNOLOGICAL ADVANTAGES OF BREAST MILK

Human milk has been found to be beneficial to the infant's immunity because it contains many components from the mother that provide immune protection to the suckling baby. These components include antibodies to infections to which the mother has already been exposed, but also to infections that have been transferred to the mother via the breastfeeding baby's saliva on the nipple. The mother's immune system recognises such foreign substances and creates specific antibodies against these invaders and transfers them back to baby through the breast milk to fight off the infection.

Additionally, human milk promotes the growth of gut-friendly micro-organisms, thereby inhibiting the growth of potentially nasty ones. This assists with the maturation of the baby's digestive system, so it will function properly in a relatively shorter time frame.[43]

These properties are also believed to be responsible for a reduction in allergies for breastfed children later on in life.

This is amazing! Our bodies are just brilliant if we let them do what comes naturally.

---

[42] Daly, S.E., Di Rosso, A., Owens, R.A. & Hartmann, P.E. *Degree of Breast Emptying Explains Changes in the Fat Content, but Not Fatty Acid Composition, of Human Milk.* Experimental Physiology 1993; **78**: 741-755.

[43] Kelleher, S.L. and Lonnerdal, B. *Immunological Activities Associated with Milk.* Adv Nutr Res, 2001; **10**: 39-65.

My firstborn started school a few weeks before my fourth child was born. As usual during the first semester, a round of Chickenpox (Varicella) went through the first year students and, two weeks later, two of my children still at home started to show symptoms. Interestingly, my baby being breastfed did not show any symptoms, so I assumed my immune system was helping to protect her.

A few years later when she started school, she didn't *catch* the Chickenpox when it passed through her first year. We didn't keep her at home, or stop her interacting with those who had it, so we concluded that while being breastfed as a baby she must have had a subclinical infection and her immune system had developed enough at that time to kick into gear when she was exposed to the same disease years later.

Bottle feed with breast milk

Bottle feeding using expressed breast milk can be a real help to the exhausted mum because daddy can take over some of the feeding sessions while mum rests. It is also necessary for any mother who chooses to return to work and still wishes to keep breastfeeding her baby. Remember to sterilize all bottles, lids and teats prior to filling. Re-heat the milk in the bottle to a lukewarm temperature by placing the bottle in a jug or cup of hot water and test it after a couple of minutes. Shake or swirl the milk gently and sprinkle a few drops onto the underside of your wrist where the skin is soft and supple. You can quickly tell if the temperature is not right. Over-heating destroys the vitamin content of the milk, so always heat it up gently. It is best not to use a microwave oven to reheat the milk because it destroys the antibodies contained in the breast milk.

The caloric fat content of expressed milk will vary depending on the stage at which the milk is expressed from the breast. If you express a 100ml volume of milk at the start of a feed session, it will have a lower concentration of milk fat than a 100ml volume expressed at the end of a feed session. So if you generally express milk at the end of a feed session, you may find that the bottled breast milk may satisfy your baby's hunger a little earlier than when feeding directly off the breast because of its higher fat content.

Bottle feed with formula milk

If you have a choice, stick with breast milk, and persist for as long as you can, even if you have to supplement your baby's feeds with formula milk. Any amount of breast milk will be beneficial to your baby. There are now some community-based websites[44] that trade in breast milk, so you can buy the milk online and have it delivered to your door. You will need to check if the service is available in your country or location.

If you have tried everything and are still unable to breast feed, then find the best formula milk available that you can afford. Formula milk has a higher caloric fat content and currently, no immunological advantage. Also, most are sourced from cow's milk, which has a completely different proportion of nutrients to human milk. Soy and goat milk equivalents are available these days.[45]

Something else of which you should be aware is that the number of fat cells in a person's body is largely determined from the age of about 30 weeks' gestation to about one year of age. During this time in a baby's development, the number of fat cells actually multiplies.[46] If the diet of the baby has a high fat content at this time, he will develop more fat cells than a baby with a balanced fat content. This may pre-dispose your child to a condition called *hyperplasia-obesity* later on in life and this type of obesity is hard to lose. After this age the fat cells do not multiply, but merely grow larger. This phenomenon can re-occur during the age of 9 to 13 years.

Make sure the bottles, lids and teats are sterilized before filling them with freshly made formula. Refrigerate all bottles until they are required and any leftover formula should be thrown out to avoid making baby sick if the milk has spoiled.

Some additional tips for feeding your baby include the mandatory bib and an extra vomit cloth. Use a clean cloth nappy or small towel under your

---

[44] Breast milk services for the USA and the UK:
www.onlythebreast.com, www.onlythebreast.co.uk

[45] Fisher, R.J., *Formulas and milks for infants and children.* Medicine Today, 2007 October; **8**(10) http://www.medicinetoday.com.au/cpd/files/articles/200710/Module%203.pdf

[46] Astrand, P.-O. and Rodahl, K., 1977, *Textbook of Work Physiology: Physiological Bases of Exercise* 2nd ed, pg 514.

baby's chin during the feed. When he's finished, gently sit him up and keep your hand under his chin to support his head. Gentle rubbing on his back with your other hand usually helps to bring up the required wind (burp). Sometimes a small amount of milk is regurgitated with the wind, so you need to have a cloth handy to catch the spills. As your baby grows larger, burping over your shoulder often ends up with the old *bird droppings* effect down your back, so always remember the catch sheet.

Remember that when you are feeding your baby, if you are relaxed and calm, then your baby will pick up on those vibrations and calm down as well. Feeding your new baby can be one of the most satisfying, gratifying and healthy things you can do.

Introducing other foods into your baby's diet begins around six months of age and includes foods that are easily digested, such as mashed bananas and unsweetened stewed apples. Resist all urges to add sugar into the baby's diet. He doesn't need to have it and if you leave it out, he won't develop a preferred taste for it. The food might not taste sweet to you, but that could be because you have a *sweet tooth*. The natural sugars in the fruits you prepare are enough.

As your baby grows, gradually introduce different foods and flavours. It's best if you make baby's food yourself, rather than buying commercially prepared foods. These often have a high salt or sugar content, so should be avoided. Your baby will learn to eat all types of different foods at a young age – even vegetables!

One of my friends is such great mum. She prepares all her baby's mushy food and then freezes it in portions in ice cube trays. This makes it so easy to pop out one or more portions at a time and reheat carefully it in the microwave oven, stir it up and serve it. Always test the temperature of the food before giving it to your child.

She uses foods like pumpkin, sweet potato, lentils, avocado, carrots, spinach, and broccoli, and different combinations of them. Her kids love them!

Use your imagination. Think of the fresh foods you like and prepare them for your baby. Let him taste some food on the tip of a spoon first and gauge his reaction. If he likes it, give him some more. If he doesn't, then leave it for a couple of days and try again. Your persistence with this will be worth your baby's future health.

Clean your baby's teeth

Baby's teeth will start to erupt from around six months of age. Baby will show discomfort, be unsettled, usually has red cheeks, and might develop nappy rash. He may want to feed more frequently, and need more comfort. He doesn't know what's going on, but feels pain and that makes him unhappy. Bear with him, and after a couple of weeks, the teeth should start to show.

Usually one of the lower middle teeth (incisors) comes through first and many a breastfeeding mother has experienced this firsthand. Babies like to chew on things to help the teeth emerge, such as a teething rusk, but when it's the nipple, then that can be quite painful. Sometimes mum's reaction is such a shock, it can make the baby upset and *he* starts to cry. Rather ironic for the mother who has a bleeding nipple!

Now is the time to introduce the toothbrush to the baby and the concept of good oral hygiene – that is, brushing your teeth to keep them healthy. Start with a tiny brush designed for baby that has very soft bristles. Let him get used to the idea of a brush in his mouth that is not meant to be chewed. Let him hold it and (perhaps) chew it a little, but then take it off him and gently brush the new tooth from the gum towards the end of the tooth, on both the inside and outside of the tooth. You don't need toothpaste at this early stage – it's too strong a taste for him and contains far too much fluoride.

Always reward baby with a big smile, a kiss, and soothing words of encouragement, like *Good boy, that was great! You have done so well! What a clever baby!*

Some people think that cleaning the deciduous (baby) teeth is a waste of time – after all they fall out when the permanent (adult) teeth emerge. This is completely misguided. Your child will have these baby teeth for many years and they need to be in excellent condition before the adult teeth emerge. They set the foundations for strong teeth and healthy gums for the rest of your child's life. If there is any infection present in the baby teeth, it can be transmitted to the adult teeth during the mixed dentition stage. This type of dental problem can be minimised, if not completely avoided, by setting a pattern of excellent oral hygiene. Your child needs to learn how to look after his teeth, and develop a sense of responsibility for them so that when the permanent ones arrive, he already knows how to look after them.

Bath your baby

This is one of the best times to have with your new baby because you can play in the water, make a big splash, and have fun! Just be prepared to have a watery mess around you, so extra towels may be necessary.

This is also an excellent time to start teaching baby about his body. Gently play with his hands, fingers, feet and toes, and repeat their names in a soft voice – don't expect him to repeat them back to you, though! Letting handfuls of water run over his head, shoulders and tummy will usually bring on a huge grin from baby.

It really doesn't matter where you bathe your baby, as long as he is safe and secure. When I was very small, my mum used to wash me in the kitchen sink and that worked well because it was a good height and the bench was very useful – just watch out for the taps! Modern baby baths are quite flashy with moulded designs and pretty colours. It's up to you, but you don't have to spend a lot of money on special baths that will become too small in a year's time. I used a hand-me-down plastic bath for my kids and that worked well.

No bath can support your baby while he is lying in the water. That is your job. If this is for a newborn, his head will require constant support from your hand or arm. Never leave your baby alone in a bath. If the phone rings, leave it – they will call back if it is important. If you must leave the room, then take baby with you wrapped up in a towel.

The basics you need are:

1. A sink or bath half filled with *warm* water – test the temperature with your elbow before you put baby into it. If it feels too hot, then it is! Same for too cold. Baby doesn't want to freeze, either.
2. Some gentle baby soap or oil to wash away the dirty bits. For boys who have not been circumcised, the advice has changed over the years.[47] Please refer to the Melbourne Royal Children's Hospital factsheet available on this book's website (www.instructionmanual4kids. com) for the most up-to-date information on this topic. The recommendations are to leave the penis alone and not attempt to pull back the foreskin at it does not detach until the boy is about two years old or older. When my boys were babies, I used to gently roll

---

[47] http://www.rch.org.au/kidsinfo/factsheets.cfm?doc_id=3715

back what I could of the foreskin and swish the penis in the bath water to carefully remove all debris that may have gathered under it. I felt it was important to prevent possible infections and at the very least remove any faecal matter that may have become caught under it.

3. A very soft face washer or similar sized piece of cheesecloth to use as a wash cloth.

4. A soft, clean towel already opened up beside the bath so you can lift baby straight onto it when bath time is over. You don't want to have to struggle with one hand trying to open a folded towel, while the other hand is holding a wet, slippery baby.

Exercise with your baby

There are at least two types of exercise you can do with your baby:

1. Playing physically with your baby – during nappy changing or bath time you can gently play with baby and his body. Each time you hold up his hands or feet, kiss them and say their names. Babies love to feel different types of things, so when he is awake and lying down, give him mobiles to play with so he can reach for the different shapes, colours and textures. Make sure they are easy to clean with just soap and water, and too large to be swallowed, as baby will put everything in his mouth. The rule of thumb for under three year olds is to only let them play with items larger than a 50 cent coin.

2. Taking baby with you as you physically exercise – this is really important for mums who want to get back to pre-baby size and weight. There are some great prams that look like all-terrain vehicles and it makes me really pleased when I see mums out there pushing the prams and setting a decent pace. The aerobic exercise is fantastic for mum and the sight-seeing is terrific for baby, especially as the months go by and he is old enough to hold up his head and look around.

    I used to joke about the *progressive weight training* all mums get as their babies grow, but it's true! Just make sure you swap sides when holding your little man, because you want to even up both of your sides as he turns into a *bigger* little man: It helps your back if you pick him up from the floor in a crouch position and use more leg muscles than bending over and using only your back muscles. You might like to squeeze in the pelvic floor muscles at this time as well to help keep them in shape. This is important because you will still need to do this well into their toddler stage – and they can get *very* heavy.

Socialise with your baby

Many people believe that once a baby comes along, you can kiss your social life goodbye. This is entirely up to you and how you adapt to life. Obviously, if mum has had a hard time during the delivery, or if baby has some issues that need specialist attention, then there will be a period of time after the birth that socialising just won't enter your head. With our first child, I did not want to leave the house in any way, shape or form until I had had some decent sleep and that took three months. There's no point in frightening the neighbours with some gothic mad woman stumbling about who has black eyes falling out of her head!

You will know when you are able to socialise again. To start with, it's easier to invite friends over to your house, so if baby needs to be changed or fed, then you can slip away and do it without too much fuss. When you become more logistically savvy, you may be brave enough to visit someone else. It doesn't take long to learn what you definitely *must* take with you even if, in the beginning, it feels like you're moving house each time. By the time the fourth child comes along, you usually just plonk a fresh nappy into your handbag and you're off.

TIP: Warn your friends that you will do your best to be on time, but now that junior has arrived, there will be occasions when you will be late or possibly even a no-show.

If your previous life included lots of partying and clubs, then you don't have to give it up entirely, but it's not a good place for a newborn. Really loud constant or sudden noises will not only upset your newborn, but could damage his delicate eardrums – not to mention your own! In this situation, it would be better to find a really good baby-sitter and leave bubs at home.

Mother's who are breastfeeding should not drink alcohol because it will affect the milk production and quality, and baby will suffer because of it. If you must indulge, express your breast milk and freeze it for later use by your baby. Then he won't have to drink from you until after the alcohol has passed out of your body. For the relatively short period of time a mother will be breastfeeding, it should not be an inconvenience to decline drinking alcohol especially when the lifelong advantages for the breastfed baby are so great. Your friends will understand your motives, and if they don't, then perhaps you need to consider if they really are friends. In all seriousness, parents with a newborn baby need to consider not only their own well being, but now that of the baby who is so totally reliant on them. Clubbing and loud parties should probably be left for those without young children.

Changing your mode of entertainment doesn't mean it isn't enjoyable for you or the older baby or toddler. There are many places where you can take your kids – outdoor parties, live music cafes, theme parks, and open-air festivals – and they really enjoy the day too.

One of the hardest things many women find difficult to do is to breastfeed their baby in public. This is entirely dependent on how modest each individual is and how embarrassed they may feel feeding their baby away from home. These days, there are specially allocated feeding rooms available in the larger shopping centres which provide some measure of privacy for modest mums. Alternatively, you can always express some of your breast milk into a bottle and feed him from that when you're in a public place.

When I was breastfeeding my babies, I found loose tops very practical. They may not have been the height of fashion, but that's a personal priority and it differs for everyone. One-piece outfits are completely out, unless you want to undress every time you feed baby.

I had a couple of tops that had split sides and lots of fabric so it was both easy and modest during feeding. After a while, when you both know what you're doing, baby attaches very quickly and completely and there is no more breast (sometimes less) showing than what can be seen from an average cocktail or evening dress.

Many people tip-toe around the house and speak in whispers when the baby is asleep, and expect other people to do so as well. This is just silly. Your baby will become used to the noises and will learn to sleep through them. Don't change your usual habits or mannerisms now that the baby has arrived. This will cause trouble down the track, so just do the same stuff as you used to do, make the same noise as usual, and baby will adapt. He may be a new family member, but he isn't the *boss*! Remember, he was in the womb for nine months and probably heard the same noises during the last month of the pregnancy, if a bit muted. I used to be amazed at what some babies could sleep through. In fact, some used to be more unsettled if there was no noise. If the room was too quiet, they would wake up and wonder where everyone was and start to cry.

Babies get used to socialising with other people. This gives them a healthier outlook on life as they learn that there are many good people in the world in whom they can have trust and respect. A well-adjusted baby is one who is happy to be nursed or cuddled by those his parents trust. Clingy babies are often ones who have picked up on a parent's nervousness and insecurity, and they feel unsure and, hence, unsafe with someone else.

Travel with your baby

Most babies love to travel – it soothes them and rocks them to sleep in no time. In fact, many worn out parents put baby in the car capsule, start the engine, and drive around the block just to put junior to sleep, then come home and put him to bed. Sounds a bit crazy, but it works!

Safety is an issue when travelling with baby, so always keep his capsule or seat secured in the back seat of your vehicle by anchor bolts and untwisted straps. If you're unsure of how to fit the capsule or seat, you may be able to visit an authorised restraint fitting station (if that service is available in your location) and have a professional, such as an ambulance officer, fit it for you.[48] It's too dangerous to have baby in the front seat, ironically because of the air bags designed to save an adult or older child. Never take short cuts with your baby's safety – there are too many cars, too much speed, and not enough driver consideration. Never drive around with someone cradling baby on their lap, or with toddlers jumping up and down on the back seat – a sure recipe for disaster.

When you are planning a shopping trip, you need to allocate time to take baby out of the car – no matter how quick you think you'll be. Many

---

[48] A list of authorised car seat and capsule fitters may be found:
http://www.crep.com.au/authorised-restraint-fitting-stations.html

parents have taken a short cut to the corner store and left baby sleeping in the car while they jump out to get a couple of things. The guilt and shame you feel when you return to the car and find your baby crying hysterically and drenched in sweat is phenomenal. Babies dehydrate rapidly, especially in summer when the interior of a car can reach 50°C or more in a very short time. It's made worse if the car is surrounded by on-lookers trying to prise open a door or window just to get your baby out. *But, it was only five minutes!* That excuse just doesn't wear well with these people. It's not worth it. No excuses – don't do it.

Taking baby on his first trip on an airline can be a complete disaster or not. You need to plan ahead and prepare according to how long the flight is going to take. Time your baby's last pre-flight feed so that he will be hungry and ready to feed when the plane is taking off and again when preparing to land. While baby is sucking and swallowing, it helps his ears adjust to the pressure changes of the cabin during the ascent and especially during the descent. This reduces any pain he may feel, and hence, minimises or prevents him crying and disturbing other passengers. You'll need to pack your cabin bag with a vomit cloth, fresh nappies (at least two), wipes, barrier cream, plastic bag for soiled items, and a change of baby clothes. Have baby's bottles handy as well, or be prepared to breastfeed in your seat. With the right top or bunny rug draped over your shoulder, this isn't a problem, as you can be very discreet. Remember that baby will react to your state of mind, so if you are calm and relaxed throughout the flight, then baby is more likely to be so as well.

Putting baby to bed

Baby's bed needs to be designed for a little person with no or limited control of his head, and if he wriggles around into the corners, he must not be able to twist things around his feet or hands in case his circulation is impeded. The mattress needs to be fairly firm so that he doesn't sink into it and you don't need a pillow or other fluffy things that could impede baby's airflow..

In the summer, a bottom sheet and cover sheet is all you need, and in winter, an additional bunny rug or two and a quilt should be enough. Baby doesn't have much strength and can't lift himself or his head out of a potentially suffocating situation, so make sure he can't put himself there accidentally. There is some great advice about putting baby to sleep on the Sids and Kids website.[49]

When you put your baby to sleep for the night (and this might be a few times each night in the beginning) get a little routine going, so baby begins to learn the pattern. Give baby a kiss and cuddle, tell him you love him, lay him on his back in bed so he can still see you and sit there for a few minutes telling him a story – any old story will do, it might even be your day at work, as long as it is told with a calm, soft voice that will help to lull baby to sleep. If you like, you can sing a song instead. I used to sing Brahms Lullaby to my babies with the following words:

Go to sleep,
Go to sleep,
Go to sleep now my darling,
Warm and cosy,
In your bed now,
You will sleep the whole night through.
In the morning you'll wake
At about 8 am,
Feeling happy and well
After sleeping all night.

OK, I know it's not poetically brilliant, but it made me feel better and put both myself and the baby in a warm and comfortable space. It's important to go to sleep feeling relaxed and peaceful. The outcomes we both needed were addressed here and I'm convinced they helped to accelerate their eventuality. Even if it's not happening just yet, keep your thoughts, speech, and feelings on the right track and it will happen. The timing is up to you. The alternative can be degrees of torture. That is also up to you.

Many people who have trouble putting their baby to sleep at night have often started out with a complication where baby has had trouble feeding properly, then holding down his food, and then not sleeping because he's still hungry or in pain and upset, and wants parental companionship constantly.

---

[49]   SIDS and Kids – safe sleeping website:
        http://www.sidsandkids.org/safe-sleeping/

Listen to the advice you get from your health care professionals[50] and your doctor. There are many dedicated websites available to assist parents – all you need to do is look for them.

A technique called *Controlled Crying* – where you place baby in his bed and gradually increase the time by one minute before you go into him, pick him up, and settle him down again – has sometimes been used, but is not recommended for babies under nine months of age. If you want to try this technique it's a good idea to warn the neighbours.

A friend of mine was trying the Controlled Crying method and had the police called on her by a well-meaning, but misguided neighbour, who could hear the baby crying a lot. Not a pleasant experience especially when you're a frazzled mum at her wits end with a baby who keeps on crying!

Many people use *dummies* or *pacifiers* to calm their babies. I didn't actually use them because I felt they were not necessary, but many mums swear by them and if it works for you, then go for it. Just remember to wash and sterilise them regularly to get rid of the germs.

When baby is asleep, watch him for a while, and then leave him alone. Resist the temptation to go in and check on him all the time – just to see if he's breathing. This will drive you nuts! Sometimes I would wake up during the night wondering about my firstborn – especially after he started to sleep through the night – and think, "Is my baby OK? Should I get up and check on him?" Then I realised that if I continued down this path, I would not be any good to anyone because I would not allow myself to have a decent night's sleep. I had to trust that things would be OK by the morning. One of the biggest things you need to learn as a new parent is to *trust* – trust yourself, trust your natural instincts, and trust the people close to you.

---

[50] The Tresillian Family Care (previously known as the Royal Society for the Welfare of Mothers and Babies) has a website with some excellent advice for parents: http://www.tresillian.net/tresillian-tips/settling-techniques-newborn-12-months.html

Actively picture and feel the best outcome

Once your baby has been introduced to the members of its new family – with all the obligatory fuss, flowers, gifts, and noise – and all the metaphoric smoke has wafted out the window, you are left feeling very alone with a tiny bundle in your arms and a huge weight of responsibility on your shoulders. Whether this bundle is one of joy, or otherwise, is entirely up to you.

"Whoa!" You declare. "That can't be right? What if the kid is just a bad egg and born to be a disobedient little so and so?"

This is just a perception and not a reality unless you make it so and that occurs in your own mind first. You don't believe me? Just think back to your first reaction to any challenging situation. Are you the type of person who looks for a solution, or do you take a mental leap to the worst possible case scenario, picture it in graphic detail and then, when it does happen, do you search high and low with the enthusiasm of a prosecuting attorney for war criminals for someone to blame? If you fall into the latter category, then you need to stop, take a deep breath, and point the blame at yourself. You need to change your initial reaction to events. This is the essence of the issue. When you focus on an outcome with a passion or with feelings of great energy, you are literally attracting the event just as you imagine – whether it be good or bad. Remember that you are the master of your own universe – your most earnest thoughts and feelings will govern your future experiences, so take control, rather than drift along aimlessly.

You need to become a person who is not just regarded as a positive thinker, but a *pro-active* thinker. This means you need to do more than just hope for the best. You need to actively picture it and feel the best possible outcome *as if it has already happened.*

For the sake of your newborn child, be a parent who not only feels a deep love for him, but who continually thinks and talks about him being a wonderful baby – one who is in perfect health and who sleeps well, feeds well and contentedly, and who is happy when awake.

Avoid guilt trips

Sometimes we feel guilty about our performance as a parent – especially with our first baby. You shouldn't. It doesn't help anyone if you are second-guessing and judging yourself all the time. Some people are *natural* parents, and some aren't. If you are doing the best you can, then that is all anyone can ask.

Over the years, there have been many time-saving devices and products appear on the market, such as disposable nappies and bottle sterilizers. Take advantage of these as much as your belief systems will allow because they can make a huge difference to how you function in the home. Washing cloth nappies is better for the environment, but sometimes it can become a massive task, especially if you haven't been able to sleep much, or if the baby is sick and needing constant support. Swapping to disposables – even for just a short time – can help you catch up and feel in control again. Another alternative is to use a nappy laundering service which provides you with clean and sanitised nappies on a regular basis for a specified price.

I always feel compassion for the first child of any new parents. They bear the brunt of the trial and error process that goes on in every household. Be gentle and forgiving with each other, because mistakes will be made.

Refer to the Instruction Manual for Kids website for updated links to all websites referenced in this book and for any others that the author believes are of benefit to parents:

www.instructionmanual4kids.com

11

Toddler Basics

Toddlers don't have an ON/OFF switch
they have a rechargeable battery!

Instructions:

1. Read the Introduction.
2. Toddler-proof your living space.
3. Teach your toddler about boundaries.
4. Speak the truth to your toddler.
5. White lies are OK if the *intent* is good.
6. It's OK to say NO.
7. Teach good manners and *do* what you *say*.
8. Kids don't hear the word DON'T.
9. Keep your sense of humour.
10. Make mundane jobs fun.
11. Toilet training will (eventually) happen.

When your toddler wakes up in the morning, he is on the go until he falls asleep, usually after lunch. Then, after about an hour's peace, he wakes up again and runs through the place like a mini-cyclone until he falls asleep after dinner and a bath. Toddlers don't tend to have fast and slow patches; it's either all on or all off – like a rechargeable battery! Then after a good night's sleep, he is recharged and ready to repeat the whole process all over again.

Toddler-proof your living space

Ever heard of the *Terrible Twos*?

Who hasn't, but just stop and think about what is happening here. What are you thinking, and hence programming, about your toddler's behaviour? Sounds like a terrible time for you both. So, don't believe it! Make it what you want from it. Change your thinking to the *Terrific Twos*. Certainly, with the usual development of kids of this age, you may feel that control is slipping away as he begins to explore the new world around him. Toddlers are naturally curious of all things within reach – and sometimes out of reach – but what is really happening at this stage is for each parent to realise they now have an increased responsibility and must be vigilant.

Accidents can happen in an instant, but the parent who is aware can reduce potential environmental impacts by *toddler-proofing* the house. Glass tables, pot plants, staircases, and so on, are all potential hazards, but they can be neutralised. For some things, such as a family heirloom or favourite ornament, it is prudent to remove it completely or place it in a very high place for a few years. This is a joint responsibility for mum and dad, so you need to agree on the strategy for proofing the home and be extra vigilant to reduce accidents and arguments. For things like staircases, while your baby is in the early crawling stage, you might like to invest in a gate to prevent access, especially at the top of the staircase. When he has developed better balance and can crawl along with relative ease, teach him how to turn around and crawl down backwards. Even go to the extent of giving him a sense of the danger here by tipping him upside down, slowly and gently, all the while holding him firmly and safely. Most babies and toddlers learn pretty quickly if you just give them a taste of the experience in a safe and controlled way.

Teach your toddler about boundaries

Toddlers need to learn that boundaries exist. The sooner they learn this concept, the happier and safer things will be. It must be taught in the home so that your toddler can understand that it exists outside of the home. I am constantly bemused by those parents who think that their toddler can do what they like at home, but then expect them to behave in a controlled way when they are at the shops, or in a restaurant, or theatre, or in another person's house.

I think just about everyone has had firsthand knowledge of the impact a screaming toddler can have on an unsuspecting public. The scenario of a little brat throwing a huge temper tantrum in a supermarket aisle usually stays with an observer for a fair while afterwards. Comments ranging from, *That kid needs a good kick up the you-know-what!* to *Can't you keep your kid quiet?* and everything in between, do nothing to assist the now-frazzled parent nor resolve the situation peacefully.

What's the best solution? Obviously, the one that works! However, depending on the child and the parent, what might work in one situation won't necessarily work in another. I heard of one parent throwing himself on the ground kicking and screaming like a three year old and that surprised his toddler so much that he stopped what he was doing and stared at his parent. Some parents try to ignore their little noise machine and continue shopping as if nothing is happening. Others try to please their toddler by offering distractions such as lollies or toys. This isn't recommended because it acts like a reward for the behaviour and actually encourages more tantrums for future outings.

> I met a man who used to throw a glass of water in his child's face whenever she threw a tantrum. It stopped the tantrum. He is now a grandfather and when his daughter confessed to him that she couldn't stop her own child from doing tantrums, he suggested she try the glass of water method.
>
> The first glass of water stopped the child who was completely surprised and shocked. Then she started to scream again. Her mother threw a second glass of water into her face, and she stopped again. But, after a brief moment, she continued screaming. Her mother then filled a jug of water and placed it near the child so she could easily see it. Not surprisingly, the child stopped screaming.

Like most of these situations, there is usually a good reason why your toddler starts to behave this way, and it is best to avoid the environment that sets it up. If the time is close to a normal feeding or sleeping time, then put off going shopping until later. If you build into your normal routine a regular shopping experience, then your child will learn to understand that only good behaviour will be tolerated. If he starts acting up in the shop, then you can take him home straight away if you are shopping alone (even if the shopping is only half done). Or, if there are two parents shopping, you can take him out to the car, strap him into his car seat, and give him a timeout of a couple of minutes while waiting out of sight behind the car.

> An excellent way to keep your toddler behaving in a shop is to keep him actively involved in the process so he isn't bored. Get him to pick out the apples and count them for you from his seat in the trolley. When he is bigger he can go to the veggies you need, so teach him to choose the best ones. He can also pick up any tins or non-breakable items as well.
>
> **TIP: When shopping with a toddler, find the basic necessities first, then if he is behaving badly, you can go home and survive. If he is behaving well, then shop for the other things you want.**

He needs to understand that actions have consequences, and certain behaviours will not be tolerated. If his action is to scream and demand things, one response is that he will be taken home, put to bed and denied the shopping outing. The next time the outing is tried, explain to him that he must be on best behaviour if he wants to come along.

> When our son was about two years old, he was very outgoing and had complete trust in the world around him. One time we were out dining at a cosy restaurant with some friends and our toddler decided to wander around the restaurant visiting the guests at the other tables. We kept a watchful eye on him to see what would happen. He didn't rush around pulling at clothes or table cloths or hand bags, instead he merely toddled up to them, looked them in the eye, gave them a big smile, and said, 'Be happy.'

**Behaviour patterns are learned
on a *daily* basis in the home.**

Repetition reinforces a type of behaviour, so make sure you are consistent with your behaviour as a parent, and that your child is getting the same message from each parent. Work out the limits and boundaries between the parents first, so you can be consistent with your child.

Speak the truth to your toddler

When kids are starting to learn and understand the spoken language, it helps if they are taught about things correctly. Some parents find it amusing to trick their kids while they are still young and gullible. As a means of amusement, this is very shallow, short-sighted, and it can erode the foundations of trust you should be building with your child. As a general rule, you should always speak truthfully to your toddler, so he can learn factual things, and also learn that his mum or dad can be relied upon to speak the truth. That is something worth having and it is important for a child to have that added safety net in his family life.

White lies are OK if the *intent* is good

The question of whether parents should *tell the truth and nothing but the truth* in every situation is often raised at Christmas time, Easter, and whenever your child loses a tooth. The myths and legends we grow up with that give us joy and enhance our well-being are generally harmless and, in some cases, can be quite beneficial.

How many kids do you know (including yourself when you were one) who chose to behave well so they could be rewarded by Santa Claus on Christmas Eve? Or who jumped up excitedly on Easter Sunday scouring the house and yard to see if the Easter Bunny had left some chocolate eggs in hidey holes? I hope you were one of the fortunate ones who received a coin as a swap for a lost baby tooth. We used to put the old tooth in a glass of water on the bedside table, and the Tooth Fairy would always come along and buy back the tooth. Incisors would cost about 10c or 20c, while a good looking molar could be worth $1. Pretty big money for a little kid who doesn't know the value or purpose of money yet!

At some point in your child's life, he will grow old enough to recognise that there's something a bit fishy going on. Like how can Santa get around to *everyone's* house across the world all in one night (or 24 hour period)? And what happens when the tooth fairy *forgets* to buy the tooth? Or why do the Easter Bunny's paw prints always smell like talcum powder? Your child should be allowed to reach this realisation in his own time before the magic of the myth escapes him forever. If we were hurt as kids, we wouldn't be so keen to pass it on to our own kids, but we generally do so because it wasn't an issue. It's just another stage of growing up and shouldn't be blown up out of proportion. Just be wary of the marketing people who love to exploit these events so they can make a quick buck. When these events are kept in perspective, they are fun and happy times, not harmful or deceitful.

Other untruths that can be considered *white lies* include the ones where your child asks you if the drawing they have done looks good. It is important for you to encourage the budding artist in all kids, so even if you can't quite make out your body – often the head is there with just the arms and legs sticking out of it – you should say something like:

Wow, sweetheart! That is really good. I can see my head so well!

Focus on the bits you can see and recognise, or just use your imagination! Kids do, so look at it from their perspective.

It's OK to say NO

It is OK to say *No* to your child. I firmly believe that too many behavioural problems are caused by the lack of that word at the right time. Neither should it be the only word he hears at this age, so you must remain calm and clear, and be prepared to let him explore the world around him, but within safe limits.

No should not be spoken in anger, but instead with assertion.

Imagine your child is about to chase a ball onto a road. All the child sees is the ball over there and he understands that he needs to go and get it. The concept of a road being potentially dangerous is totally alien to him. He has not developed mentally enough to be able to plan for that possibility. You need to know this and prepare for these situations.

In this case, you have no idea whether a car is coming, but it is best to stop your child before anything terrible might happen. Say *No* with assertion, and loudly so that he hears it. Tell him to wait at the kerb for you, then hold his hand firmly and explain about looking to both sides of the road. Turn his head with your hands if you must, but make sure he understands what needs to be done here. When the road is clear, you take him to the ball, so he can pick it up and carry it back. During this time you are controlling the situation so it is safe for your child and you are teaching him the correct way to retrieve a ball, or to cross a road when he is older. Hold hands with your child up to the age of 10 years old as he doesn't yet have the mental capacity to time the speed of an oncoming vehicle with the time it takes to cross the road safely.

Teach good manners and *do* what you *say*

Good manners need to be taught from an early age and repeated until they become second nature. The children who know how to say *Please* and *Thank You* are always regarded highly and are given respect immediately. Every time your child wants something from you, you say *please*. Every time you pass something to your child, you say *thank you*. This helps to instil a basic awareness of self-control in the young child's mind – he can't just grab something and run off; he must go through a little ritual that seems to please mum and dad.

At this young age, most kids are more than willing to do things to please their parents, and sometimes you can reward him for his good behaviour, such as with a favourite piece of fruit or some extra special play time with mum. (Sorry, lollies are OUT!) Rewards are great and work well as long as they are infrequent. If you reward your child too often, it becomes an expectation on each occasion and it loses its value. Your child may then throw a tantrum because he didn't get a reward. He needs to learn that it is based on the discretion of the parent whether he deserves the reward, and just because he wants it, doesn't mean he will get it.

It is important to *do what you say* as well. Your toddler is learning so much during these years and much of it is at the behavioural level. Parents need to be absolutely consistent with their behaviour and if you say you will do something, then you must do it. If you don't, then your child will be confused and start to doubt your word. This starts to build the beginnings of mistrust. It is important not to ridicule your toddler or make fun of him in any way, even if you think it is harmless. It's not. Your toddler will suffer the pangs of shame and confusion – *what have I done?* Never put your child in this position. It may set him up for victimisation later on in life and nobody wants that.

Always show complete love and consideration for your toddler so that he can grow up with his innocence intact.

Kids don't hear the word DON'T

Children don't hear the word DON'T. They have highly fertile and imaginative minds and operate using vivid pictures. Let me illustrate this with a simple example.

> When our son was three years old, he had been eating a jam sandwich at the table and got off his chair to walk into the kitchen to wipe his hands. I knew this; my husband knew this; but my mother did not.
>
> She said, 'Don't wipe your hands on the wall!'
>
> Well, guess what he did? He straight away turned to the wall and wiped his hands on it! He had never done this before and was quite confused at then being scolded for doing precisely what he had been instructed to do.

What you say to them paints a picture in their mind. It's like saying *don't think of a pink elephant*. What do you see? A pink elephant! That's why *No Smoking*, *Speed Kills* or *Lose Weight* messages fail. They are focussing on the wrong thing. They should be *Breathe Fresh, Clean Air Only, Drive Relaxed and Live* or *Healthy Bodies.*

One of the most common phrases you will hear just about any parent from anywhere in the world say is *I told you so!*

Why do you think that is accurate? Because the parent has already painted the picture for the child to absorb and then act out just as it was described to them.

Johnny, don't stand on that wall, or you'll fall off and really hurt yourself.

Then, after the child does exactly what he has been instructed to do, the parent, very annoyingly, says *Why did you do that? I told you what would happen. I told you so.* Exactly!

So, when you are instructing your child, see the pictures your words are creating and make sure the picture is the same as the outcome you want. If it isn't, then change it!

Keep your sense of humour

A healthy sense of humour is vital for any parent. Always keep a stack of good comedies around that you can watch when you're feeling low, unhappy or about to lose control. Or perhaps you have a funny photo that always makes you smile. Look at it until you can feel the tension in your brow release and a smile or laugh has transformed your face. This is important! You cannot be an effective parent if you're stomping around the house, or banging pots and pans with furrowed brows and a thunder cloud hanging over your head. Lighten up and stop taking yourself so seriously.

When I felt like that, I used to think that there's always someone in the world worse off than me, so what have I got to complain about? In later years, I have evolved this thought to include strong feelings of gratitude and thanks for all the wonderful things I have in life, including my amazing family, animals, and the environment in which I live. This takes away the heaviness almost immediately and puts a smile back on my face. Try it, it works.

If you don't have a sense of humour yet, then where have you been? Find it now because it's going to be a huge asset for the rest of your life.

I'm convinced there is some corollary of Murphy's Law[51] that is specific for kids and animals. Invariably, if you're running late for something

---

[51] Murphy's Law: If a thing can go wrong, it will!

important, something else will happen to make you even later. Baby will throw up all over his or his sibling's new clothes, or the dog will jump up and spill the cake you've just spent an hour making. If you were a fly on the wall observing all this, you would probably laugh yourself silly, but when you're in the middle of it, the humour escapes you until later, or if you have a more serious temperament, you might not find it amusing at all.

To maintain your sanity, you just have to relax – sometimes sitting on the floor helps – look for the funny side, laugh about it, and make any necessary phone calls so other people are not going to worry about your absence. Then pick yourself up, clean up the mess, and keep moving forward.

Make mundane jobs fun

There will be many jobs you need to do, with and around your toddler. If you look for the fun in each job, then you can make the time pass quickly and the job more enjoyable.

Packing up doesn't have to be a chore if you make it a race to see who can pack away the most toys in a minute or an exercise in skills – if the toys are all robust, then they can be lobbed into a waiting toy box or basket. Count each toy with your toddler as it disappears into the box. Who knows, a budding basketball star may be just waiting to grow up!

When I needed to clean my kids teeth, I used to make-believe there was a tiny rabbit hiding in their mouths. He would jump behind each tooth and I would try and catch him with the brush. When I couldn't see well enough, the kids would open their mouths as wide as they could. This gave me a perfect view of their teeth as they were so willing to hold their heads back and open their mouths.

This was a fun time and the kids really enjoyed it. Even in their early teens, they would sometimes ask me to clean their teeth with the 'bunnies'.

The best part is they all have brilliant teeth with little or no fillings.

Give yourself extra time to do the jobs with your kids. If you are used to running around doing things with the stopwatch going, then throw it away. Time means nothing to kids and when you are with them, you need to understand that, otherwise you will give yourself unnecessary stress and create an unfriendly environment.

If you haven't already started reading stories to your kids, now is a great time to do it. They really love it and if you set a precedent that is based on good behaviour, you will have willing kids motivated to do the right things at bedtime. Don't deny them the story as a punishment because this is a great way to finish off the day in a loving and nurturing way. Rather, use an extra story as a reward for good behaviour.

TIP: Use the CARROT, not the Stick approach with toddlers.

Toilet training will (eventually) happen

Many parents get caught up in the race to have their child toilet trained first among their peers. This is one of the first types of competition about your kid that you can enter without necessarily realising until you're already in the middle of it. Others include such things as the crèche/pre-school/ school he goes to, the clothes he wears, his favourite toy, and so on. As soon as you become aware of it, back off from it, and let your kid develop and grow at his own pace.

If you feel motivated, by all means read all there is to know about toilet training and try a few things. Just remember that there are physiological stages which have to be reached before any child will be able to recognise and control his urge to urinate or defecate. There are voluntary and involuntary control mechanisms in place and the toddler must have developed enough for the whole system to work. If things aren't working for you, stop trying and let a couple of months pass before trying again. When the time is right, it will happen quickly and permanently.

My son was nearly four years old and still needed to use night nappies. We had tried a number of things – none of which worked – so in the end, we let him be, hoping he would grow out of them before he started school.

His younger sister was coming up to two years of age and was a fast learner. She was beginning to understand about the potty and its use already.

> I'm not sure whether the realisation that his little sister might be trained before he was motivated him more than anything else we tried, but the result was he was able to give up nappies entirely about two weeks before his little sister!

A large amount of stress is self-induced, but as a parent you have an entirely new potential source of stress – and I mean *potential* in all seriousness. Over the years, I observed many mothers and fathers stressing out over inconsequential things, such as whether their child is better than someone else's, or what other people will think of them, or whether they have given their child enough love? With regard to the first question, it is completely arbitrary, totally judgemental, and should never be given a second thought. The next one falls into the *who cares?* category. And as far as the last is concerned, *love* is not measurable. It either exists or it doesn't and the difference is quite noticeable – like the light being on or off. You love your child. That is a truth, so don't fret about it. Just show your love in meaningful ways with lots of cuddles, loving words, good guidance, and discipline when it is required.

12

Pre-teen Basics

You are your child's role model.

Instructions:

1. Read the Introduction.
2. Spend quality time with your kids.
3. Make pack up time fun.
4. Teach your child about good personal hygiene.
5. Teach your child how to think.
6. Keep your language clear and polite.
7. Encourage continuing good manners.
8. Teach your child about sharing and responsibility.
9. Encourage, encourage, encourage

The Pre-teen years are arguably the most important formative years for your child. He is probably somewhere between four (4) and twelve (12) years of age, is generally quite well coordinated and he absolutely loves you being involved in his activities. He will usually be attending some form of pre-school or school; will generally still allow you to kiss him goodbye at the gate; and will want you to come into the classroom periodically to help out the teacher, himself, or other class mates.

Like it or not, you are up on a pedestal of his creation and in his eyes, you can do little wrong. Obviously, the timing and situation for each child will vary, but for the vast majority of (dare I say) normal families with normal relationships (that is, loving, trusting, and respectful ones), you, as parents, are some of the major players in your child's world. Other people with whom your kids may want to align include their school teachers, close family friends, and other family members, such as uncles, aunts or cousins. Role models have changed over the last couple of generations. Traditionally, the men were the bread-winners of the family, while the women stayed at home and raised the kids. Now-a-days, this black and white, highly regimented structure is masked in a myriad of shades of grey and there are many variations of the family structure. This is not a bad thing, as it allows for the possibility of more flexible parenting and sharing with your child.

Spend quality time with your kids

Now is the time to cement those lifelong memories we all hope to have and to build strong relationships with the younger generation. Plan your work time carefully so that you have a balanced amount of time to spend on personal activities. This will help prevent you ignoring family time because it may not be seen as important as work time – I mean, after all, you don't get paid for family time, do you? This is a classic excuse, but it couldn't be further from the truth. The payment you receive is a composition of the lifelong memories; the enduring love and respect for each other; and the feelings of joy and happiness not able to be purchased by any amount of money. This is your true wealth because it feeds your very spirit, and that of your child. The capital investment in your child's self-esteem, memories, and experiences is priceless.

With the younger kids, set aside a specific time each day to spend with them and them only. This may be quite difficult if you have many siblings still at home, so if you are organising an activity with the entire group, make sure you spend about the same amount of time with each child. Set the activity for each child appropriately; don't expect as much intelligent thinking or coordinated behaviour from a two year old as you would from a four year old.

Have a variety of activities that can support a range of ages, such as building blocks, toy animals, toy trucks, trains, and cars. Encourage the imagination of your child by introducing the concept of the world and the countries that make it up. Show him large puzzles of the world and talk about the animals that live in each as you help him put the puzzle together. Introduce new concepts about the world we live in as you play with him, such as road safety while playing with the cars and trucks, and on which side of the road we drive – learning what is left and what is right is a concept with which some adults still have difficulty!

When your pre-teen is in the latter stages of this period, he and any siblings can become involved in activities that will teach them further life skills, such as caring for the environment around them. Any respect they can learn at this stage will be the basis for a love of the world around them and help to make them responsible citizens.

A great activity to do with your kids is to teach them how to make a compost heap. This may be a little difficult if you live in an apartment building, but you may still be able to organise something after discussions with the building's body corporate, or a sympathetic neighbour. All you need is a piece of land about one square metre in size. The bin itself can be home-made or bought at a garden store with full instructions about what to do and what not to do. One thing to remember is to exclude meat from the compost as this will attract rodents, such as rats. Also, if you want lots of worms, you will need to exclude citrus peels and onions, as they discourage their presence.

Once it is in place, explain about the way food starts to decompose after a few days (unless it is a well-known hamburger bought from a well-known fast food restaurant, in which case it takes *months* to decompose) and it returns to the basic building blocks from which all life is created. It may look and smell disgusting, but the worms and other saprophytic[52] creatures love it. In your kitchen, get your children to pick out a container that would be suitable for a receptacle of all your food scraps, let them write *COMPOST* on it, and put it where the family pet can't get into and mess up, such as on the bench or in a cupboard near the sink. When the container is getting full, or the first thing in the morning before school, take your kids out to your compost bin with one of them carrying the container (make a roster if they start to argue about whose turn it is). Get them to lift the lid and throw in the contents. Have a look around and discuss what you can all see. Explain that as the bin becomes fuller and more decomposition goes on, it starts to look like just dirt in there, but really rich and dark brown in colour. This means it is really healthy and nutritious for plants, and just perfect for pot-plants or a vegetable garden – the next idea for an activity with the kids. If your compost bin is looking a little sad, why not find out the reason with your child, and in the process teach them how to research things using the internet – another great activity and learning experience.

When young kids understand the reason for doing something, they take it on board absolutely. At this age, they usually love to help make the world a better place, so encourage it.

The favourite bedtime ritual of reading a story to your kids should be well-entrenched by this time. But now that your pre-teen is of school age and learning to read, get him to read a simple book to you each night. This will help him with his own learning processes and in preparation for later years. As he progresses, choose books that will challenge him a little, but not too hard that they discourage him.

It may be that work commitments keep you back late at night, but try to keep these to a minimum. These *meetings* you have scheduled with your kids should be set in concrete rather than sand because they are too important to put off to another time.

---

[52]   An organism that lives on decaying material.

I can still remember the times my dad used to take us kids to bed. I loved to be carried (sometimes using the fireman's lift, and sometimes all three at once, before we grew too big) and then have a story read to us. Sometimes, if dad was tired, he just made up a quick story out of his head. Other times, we would ask for a particular favourite.

Then we would say our prayers, and dad would tuck us in and kiss us goodnight on the forehead. It was so special.

Make pack up time fun

Packing up everything after an activity is finished should be done as a shared activity with both the parent and the child participating. The earlier your child learns that this is the normal routine, the more usual the behaviour will become and this avoids irresponsible actions and avoidance later on in life. The behaviour is reinforced at school, so they should know it at home, too.

Initially, it may make the packing up task slower because there is a lot of double handling, but it is well worth it, so make sure there is plenty of extra time to complete it. Remember the story of the famous English nanny and the spoonful of sugar to help the medicine go down? Well, the philosophy works here as well – perhaps not the spoonful of sugar bit, but if you make the time fun, then it's just like another activity for your child. When you do it with him – feeling relaxed and happy, not rushed and angry – he'll love it and that's all the reward he needs.

Don't expect him to do the pack up perfectly the first or even the tenth time, but just get him into the idea that one process follows after another – pack up follows after the play session – and they can all be fun times. If you explain the logic that you can't play trains with him until the blocks are packed away because there's no room on the floor, then he can understand why it must be done. If you still need to clean up, do it later when your child is not present, rather than taking over from him at that time, otherwise he may begin to feel that he can't do it properly and lose confidence in his ability. Continually encourage him as he does it, and get him to improve with each additional session. Eventually, he should be able to do the pack up by himself.

Scenario: Painting Session

For example, when cleaning up after a painting session, the parent should pass all the equipment to be cleaned (one by one) to the child to wash in the sink, such as the brushes, the rinsing jar, any cloths, etc. Explain that the brushes need to be washed really well by rinsing out all the paint. This makes them last longer and they will be good to use next time. If the paint isn't washed out, then the brush will harden up and not be able to be used. If you have an old brush, you might like to experiment with it and leave the paint in it. The next time you have a painting session, your child will be able to see the result of not cleaning up properly. Keep the brush in a prominent position each time you have a painting session as a visual reminder. These images can leave a lasting impression on a child's mind and provide a clearer and more forceful message than using words alone.

Pack up time is vitally important as it serves to pass on a sense of responsibility to the child. He soon learns to recognise that along with the right to be able to do a play activity comes the responsibility of packing or cleaning up so that the right to do that activity will exist again on another day.

Teach your child about good personal hygiene

Once your child has reached the pre-teen years, he will want to be a little more independent and that should be encouraged gradually with age. If he wants to play outside with the dog, the garden, or outside toys, he needs to understand that when he has finished, he needs to clean his hands and get rid of all the dirt and germs that may have gathered on them. It's easy to see dirt because it's brown or black, but micro-organisms aren't visible to the naked eye, so you need to explain to your child about these tiny little bugs that have the potential to make people very sick. If your child handles coins or money, that can also be a very dirty activity and he needs to wash his hands thoroughly after touching money, too.

Then there is the toilet. Once your child has been trained to use the toilet (anywhere from two to four years old and more) that is a great advancement in your child's life – and your own! While your child is still young, teach him to sit on the toilet seat and wait until he has completely finished.

> I didn't tell my boys to stand up and urinate, they just figured it out as they grew up and as their exposure to school and public toilets and urinals increased. This helped to keep the toilet floor at home a little cleaner with less drips!
>
> Then there is the argument about the toilet seat being left raised up. We didn't have that problem because I taught my kids to always close the lid before they flush. This helps prevent the spread of airborne particles (bugs in tiny drops of moisture) that are launched into the air every time someone flushes. Let's face it, who wants their toothbrush covered in micro-droplets of toilet water! Preventing this is basic good hygiene.

Public toilets are another place where your kids (and you) can pick up a myriad of bugs and potential diseases. I taught my kids to always wipe the seat with a few sheets of paper before tearing off a couple of sheets at a time and covering the seat with paper so there is a physical barrier between your skin and the seat. Then if you need to do No. 2 (poo), you can put some more paper in the bowl to avoid splashes. For boys who only want to do No. 1 (wee), then there are urinals, which are quicker and easier to use, but girls don't have that luxury. When washing hands, I would always wash the tap with soap as well as my hands because germs are put on it when you turn it on, and also from everyone else who has used it before you – who knows where their hands have been? The more modern facilities have timed or sensor taps so you don't have to touch anything. I applaud the forward thinking planners for this, and also the ones who create door free entries. Door handles are such a trap. You need to wait until someone comes in and escape out before touching anything, or use a paper towel or a spare tissue on the handle to open the door and throw it in a bin somewhere outside the toilets – there usually is one. These places always make me feel grateful that I have a good immune system.

> **WARNING**: Many marketers would have us believe that anti-bacterial hand washes are going to save us from picking up diseases. This is just wrong. They kill off a high percentage of bugs, but not all, and the ones they can't kill off are usually the more virulent ones

that make you seriously ill. Good hygiene habits in combination with a perfectly functioning immune system, and good genetics will help you fight diseases. You can't help your genetic inheritance, but you can give your body the best possible chance of coping with disease by feeding and exercising it properly, allowing a degree of exposure to common bugs through normal daily activities, and then maintaining hygienic habits to minimise your exposure to the bad bugs.

At a bare minimum, ensure your kids always wash their hands thoroughly before eating food. Teach them by showing them how to do it with your hands, then with theirs, and when they understand what to do, watch them as they do it themselves and when they do it correctly, tell them how great they are and what a good job they've done. They have learned an important lesson and they should be congratulated for it. Instilling habits of good personal hygiene into your child while they are young will help to minimise potential sickness and disease for life.

Keep your language clear and polite

Kids in the pre-teen years are usually extremely innocent, gullible, and impressionable. These are the years where everything you do is being monitored by them. They take things quite literally, so be careful with what you say. A child's perspective is quite different from that of an adult for the simple reason that they don't have the worldly experience most parents possess. When you speak with your child about things, remember his ignorance at this level and guide him with a clear and gentle speech that is neither condescending nor patronising.

Your pre-teen might ask you a simple question like *Why do you go to work every day?* It is a straight-forward question and one that a young child might not understand. You might be sarcastic and cynical, and reply:

Are you kidding? I go to work every day to earn enough money to pay all the bills that just keep flowing in the mail. I go to work just so you can eat and have all the toys and things you like. I also work so your mother can go out and spend lots of money on clothes and trinkets that she doesn't really need.

This could create feelings of shame for his ignorance because he doesn't yet understand the concept of *money*, *bills* and *payments* (and what a *trinket* is);

it could teach him that sarcasm may be a valid way to communicate with people, especially loved ones; and it could start an awareness of discontent between the parents, leading to insecurity and uncertainty. This is setting up a potential hot spot for all sorts of issues, including sibling rivalry and relationship issues in later years.

Instead, answer your innocent pre-teen with a gentle and honest answer, something like:

Sweetheart, I go to work every day so I can earn a thing called money. Money is very useful because everyone in the whole world can use it to buy things they need, like food and clothing. If there is any left over, it can be saved up. When a person has worked a long time, he might have saved up enough of it to buy a really big thing, like a house. So, I work every day so I can get some really special things in life for you and your mother. You are very special to me and I want to do that for you both.

This type of reply is not only teaching your pre-teen some facts about life as an adult, but also reassuring him that he is loved and secure.[53]

> A colleague tried various approaches with his two-year old daughter and what worked for him was linking the concept to a single known 'treat (in his case, a babycino.[53]) Once his daughter understood the connection between having money and being able to get more babycino, she figured out the rest really quickly (too quickly, from her dad's perspective!)

Because you have been open and honest with him, he will know that he can trust what you say and, at some time in the future, he may be able to tell some of his friends about the concepts he has just learned from you, without the fear of being wrong and hence ridiculed.

> A colleague of mine was having trouble with her young son at school. He was being made an 'example' by his teacher for his uncooperative behaviour and lack of obedience in class. His behaviour had been explained to his parent by the teacher in front of the whole class, so he was made to feel embarrassed and ridiculed.
>
> What caused the apparent obstinate behaviour was a misunderstanding about a pencil. His teacher had stated at the beginning of the session that everyone only had *one* pencil to use for the exercise. Soon after the

---

[53] A small cup of frothy milk that looks like a cappuccino, only without the coffee.

commencement of the task, this boy's pencil broke, so he then refused to do any more work. His *literal* understanding combined with his lack of self-confidence prevented him from explaining to his teacher about the broken pencil, because he felt he could not get another one, but also, he would be in trouble for breaking the first one even though it was broken accidentally.

The teacher was not responsive enough to realise he may have another issue underlying his *behavioural* response. If she had chosen to investigate the problem a little further, without causing shame, fear, and guilt upon the boy, she may have been able to resolve it much earlier.

Always ask your child what he has learned in the day, especially when he has been at school. Then if any little issues or problems have been raised in his mind, you can discuss it with him and explain ways to deal with it before it has the potential to develop into something more serious.

I found dinner-time around the table extremely useful for finding out about any current issues. I would ask the kids what was the *best* thing that happened to them that day. Usually, one of the four would have something really interesting to share with the rest of us. Then, because the conversation had been started with something positive, invariably everyone else would open up with other things that had occurred. They had been given a chance to think about their day and search for some good points.

Sometimes, a frustration or problem might be voiced at this time because the incident had been resurrected during the thought process. This was always good because everyone could hear what happened and voice their opinion as well. This discussion allowed the younger ones to experience more of the world through their siblings' eyes, and additionally, allow the older ones to hear honest and potentially unbiased comments from others.

It is important to keep a good relationship with your kids' teachers because they are such an important influence on your child. Enjoy a little chat with them before or after school and make certain they know you are interested in what is happening in the classroom at all levels. Teachers are usually very grateful for the interest shown by parents, especially if there are problems – whether learning or behavioural.

If you are in the position to volunteer in your child's classroom, then do it. This will make your child feel special because of your particular attention to him and to show you off a bit in front of his peers. You also learn more about the class dynamics and can explain to him about the behaviour of other kids in the class – there will always be the distracters, bullies, and teacher's pets. Sometimes there may be children with special needs, such as visual impairment, which may need to be discussed with your child to enable him to understand the issues the visually challenged child must face daily. The classroom is a mini-world and many life lessons can be learnt within it. Discussing these differing personalities or difficulties without judgement or bias can help to teach your child about tolerance and consideration for others and that it takes all types to fill this world – *difference* doesn't necessarily mean *bad*, it just needs understanding.

There was a boy at my kid's school who was blind and had a Guide Dog to help him navigate around the school. All the kids in the school loved this dog, but weren't allowed to play or feed him because that would affect his training and hence his ability to steer his young master in the right direction.

The Vice-Principal happily confided in me one day, saying, "Having a Guide Dog in the school is the best thing we could've done to keep the litter problem down."

All the kids in the school had been told to make sure they bin all their rubbish just in case the dog picked it up and ate it, which was to be avoided, if possible. This not only helped the boy keep his dog healthy, but helped the school keep clean and tidy!

Teach your child how to think

Children between the ages of nine and eleven years old are ideal to teach how to think because they have developed enough to be able to focus on a topic for a specific period of time and they have not yet felt the sting of embarrassment too many times if they say something wrong.[54] They love to play games and enjoy learning new things. As the expression goes, *strike while the iron is hot!*

Children can have such fertile imaginations, and it is part of your job as the parent to encourage them to think and imagine things beyond the mundane or the usual. Be spontaneous and allow your kids to be so as well.

---

[54] de Bono, E. *Teach Your Child How To Think*, 1992; pg 32.

If everything is planned to the letter, there is no room for spontaneity, so make sure you allow time for spontaneous activities as well as, or during, the planned ones.

Encourage your child to use his imagination by playing a different character. Role playing is an excellent way of stimulating young imaginations. It doesn't have to be the traditional roles either. Playing animal characters is just as much fun (if not more) as pretending to be a specific career type, such as a nurse or tightrope walker.

One of the first ways to encourage your child to think is to ask him specific questions about a topic. Then if he comes up with an answer, always thank him for it and if it is not really heading in the right direction, suggest he might like to think of an alternative. If he is having trouble, gently point him in the right direction by suggesting further possibilities. You can do this by asking open questions that require him to give a thoughtful answer, rather than a simple *yes* or *no*.

Dr. Edward de Bono is a world-renowned educator of his own original thinking concepts and practices for individuals, businesses, and foreign and public affairs. His background in psychology and medicine has placed him a unique position to be able to teach his varied methods for activating the thinking processes in people. I particularly like two of his methods, which are suitable for pre-teens. These are called C&S (Consequence and Sequel – we will focus only on Consequence here) and PMI (Plus, Minus, and Interesting).[55] Probably one of the easiest ways of explaining these methods is using an example. One of the most common questions any parent will be asked at some time in their child's pre-teen years is *Can I have a pet?*

The usual response from the parent is something like:

No! What do you want a pet for? It's too much trouble. You'll get sick of it after a week and then we'll be stuck with it. You'll always be spending money on it; not only for food and equipment, but what if it gets sick? The vet bills will be exorbitant! What if YOU get sick? Then I'll have to look after your pet.

And so on. It's not a pretty conversation with the child on one side whinging and complaining about how the parent never lets him get anything he wants, and the parent on the other side refusing to be talked into a relatively serious commitment.

An alternative would be to answer your child with something like:

Well, let's do a C&S and a PMI on it to see if it's a possibility.

---

[55]   de Bono, E. *Teach Your Child How To Think*, 1992; pg 124-130.

Then, instead of destroying your child's hopes with all the reasons why it cannot be done, let him think of the answers to your well-directed questions. The first concept your child needs to understand is that having a pet in the house will have *Consequences* that will impact the whole family.

For your child, it means an increased responsibility to care for and consistently attend to his pet every day and possibly many times a day. He needs to understand this and be aware that even if he is busy or feeling a little unwell, he still needs to perform, at a minimum, the very basic daily task of feeding his animal. He must sincerely agree that this is his responsibility and his alone. If he cannot attend to his animal, then he must find someone to substitute for him during his absence. As soon as he is present or well enough, he must take on the full responsibility again. If he cannot agree to this, then there is no point in continuing with the discussion.

The rest of the family will be impacted to a greater or lesser degree and the *Consequences* needs to be determined for each member. So, ask your child how he thinks mum, dad, and any siblings may be impacted. He will probably not want any younger siblings to touch his pet until they are old enough to be a potential substitute carer, after which time, they could be quite useful. Mum and dad will be the providers of food, a safe environment, and any health care for the pet. So, he may need to do some chores around the house to cover these costs. Depending on your child's age, he may be able to do simple things like picking up his dirty clothes and taking them to the laundry, or keeping his room tidy, or putting the remote control next to the TV. You will need to determine what your child is capable of doing and then raise the bar a little higher, so he extends beyond his *comfort zone* a little to achieve it.

Also, if there is already a pet in the house, such as an older dog or cat, ask him what he thinks the *Consequences* might be for it. It may cause the older animal a greater degree of stress, or introduce a dominance struggle between the two competitors resulting in fighting, or it might make the older animal become more active again and feel fitter and younger.

So, the *Consequences* of your child wanting to have a pet include such things as him doing a lot more work around the home to help out mum and dad, as well as an added effort to care for his new pet.

If there is still a keenness to have a pet, make a list of all the potential pets he would like, and then help him think of as many *positive* (Plus), *negative* (Minus) and *Interesting* points as you can about each pet. If necessary, suggest an example of each point and then let your child try to do the same. The obvious *Pluses* may include such things as a warm and furry pet to cuddle which makes him feel happy and good (unless he chooses a snake or spider). The *Minuses* are generally all the added responsibilities, including putting up with the smell of their cage or living area if it hasn't been cleaned out for a while. An *Interesting* point may include such things as the interest he receives from friends or family. It may make him feel more important because he can cope with these new challenges in his life. If he takes his puppy for a walk, he might meet new people who love dogs as well, and they may say hello to him every time they see him and his dog. If he has an ant farm, it may be of interest just to sit and watch the ants dig burrows and tunnels in the sand and wonder what they are thinking of as they work, or whether they do think.

If the *Minus* points have not yet overpowered the *Plus* points, then the next question could be: *What type of pet would suit us and our current situation?* If you live on a boat, then a rabbit or guinea pig might not be a good choice, as they need fresh grass to eat. If you live in an apartment, then you need to find out whether the body corporate of the building allows for pets, and if so, for which types or breeds. If you live in your own house, then a lot more options are usually available to you. Give your child the pertinent facts and then ask him to find the answers:

We live at the top of a cliff, with a pool filling the entire back yard. The only grass we have is a small patch at the front door and we have no front fence. Your mother is allergic to cat fur and is a stickler for the house being spotlessly clean. Which type of pet animal do you think we could have and allow us to keep our current lifestyle?

Each time your child mentions a type, you can remind him of the PMI points and the Consequences:

C: *Can we have a puppy?*

P: *Well, let's think where can we keep it?*

C: *How about the back yard?*

P: *Do you think so? Is there any room for it there?*

C: *No, I guess not. What about in my bedroom?*

P: *Do you think mummy will agree to that? You know how much she loves a clean and tidy house.*

C: *No, I guess not. What about in the laundry?*

P: *Well, maybe as a puppy, but if it grows too big it won't fit in there anymore. Do think it would like to run around and have space to dig and chew a bone?*

C: *Yes, I guess so.*

P: *Do we have space outside for that kind of thing?*

C: *Not really.*

P: *Well, let's think of a different pet.*

C: How about a kitten?

And so it goes on. You can use the same type of questioning and responses for each new pet type. In the end, you may decide a fish in a bowl is all that is required or possible at this stage. Remember, your sanity is also at stake.

At face value, this exercise may appear to be rather long and tedious, but be aware that you have engaged your child in both the thinking and the decision-making processes. These are life skills that he will remember, especially if you encourage him to repetitively use these methods for everyday challenges.

The other amazing point to this process is that you have spent an amazing amount of time with your child to help him reach an agreed solution. He will be happy that you have invested that time with him; he knows he is important to you; and he knows where he fits in the household structure. It is a very stabilising and rewarding experience.

Encourage continuing good manners

The foundations of good manners that you have introduced with your child as a toddler need to be reinforced and expanded with the pre-teen. Many of the manners and common etiquette of previous generations appears to be forgotten or ignored and could easily be considered a threatened species these days. This is a great pity because a polite and civilised society will always accept a polite child into its midst. There are many aspects of daily life where good manners are welcome and these include some of our simplest communications:

Salutations:	"Good morning, mum."	*To any family member or close friend, spoken lightly and happily.*
	"Good night, dad."	*To any family member or close friend, spoken with love and respect.*
	"Hello, how are you?"	*To new or distant acquaintances, and actually listen to the response so you can continue the conversation based on their response.*

	"Bye," or "See you later."	*To farewell family or friends.*
	"Goodbye. It was nice to meet you."	*To farewell a new acquaintance.*
Answering the telephone:	"Hello, this is *Lisa*. How can I help you?"	*Substitute your name and always be polite.*
	"No, thank you."	*If it's a random caller, be polite and hang up. It's usually just their job.*
Regarding things:	"May I please have ..." or "May I have ... please."	*Whenever you want something from someone else.*
	"Thank you very much."	*Whenever you receive something from someone else.*
	"Yes, of course you can."	*Whenever someone asks you for something that you can give them.*
	"That's my pleasure."	*Whenever someone thanks you for something that you gave them.*
	"Bless you."	*After someone has sneezed.*
	"Thank you for asking."	*If someone has shown unsolicited verbal consideration to you.*

I have observed that if good manners are displayed by at least one adult, then others (especially children) will notice it and usually start displaying the same traits. This is a win-win for everyone.

Your pre-teen should be eating meals at the table, so proper table manners should be taught and encouraged. Getting him to help set the table is a great way of teaching him the fork is on the *left*.

TABLE MANNERS

Basic table manners include setting the table correctly. The usual cutlery setting is a fork, knife, soup spoon, and dessert spoon. Other forks, knives, and spoons may be added but this depends upon the number of courses you will be eating. In general, the outside cutlery is used first and

---

you work your way inwards with each new course. The fork is placed on the left of the plate and the spoons and knife are to the right of the plate. The soup spoon is on the right of the knife and the dessert spoon is placed to the left of the knife (sometimes it is placed above the head of the plate, though usually this is when paired with a small cake fork and at a formal function).

The dinner setting will include a dinner plate, sometimes a small side plate (to the left of the fork) for a bread roll, a glass (slightly to the right and above the knife and spoons) and a serviette (usually folded over and placed on top of the side plate).

If you're confused by now, imagine how a child must feel! That's why repetitive practice is essential.

When the TV is off (an absolute necessity), everyone is seated, and the dinner has commenced, one of the first lessons to learn is how to use the cutlery correctly. They should not be used in such a way as they are being *strangled*. You usually hold the implements with your hand on top; palm facing downwards and each handle is actually in the palm of your hand. The soup spoon is an exception, because the palm is upward and you take a spoonful of soup from the back of the bowl, rather than the front. The fork secures the food as it is cut by the knife. Some people seem to want to just rip the food apart, rather than using the knife in a sawing motion. You lose less food around the plate or on the floor if you practice sawing the food with the knife. Push the food onto the back of the fork with the knife. Take the fork to your mouth, not the other way around.

Smaller mouthfuls are much nicer than large ones. For starters, you can fit the whole thing into your mouth without sharing food with the table. Then it is easier to keep your lips shut while you chew the food, thus avoiding sharing your food with everyone around you! If you chew and swallow the entire mouthful before you prepare the next one, this allows you time to eat and digest your meal more slowly and comfortably.

When you are having a conversation during dinner, ensure you have swallowed all the food in your mouth before you start to speak. Other people do not like to see the half-masticated bits falling out of your mouth as you speak. That is considered quite bad manners. And if you are trying to emphasize a point in the discussion, waving your cutlery around like a pirate rattling his sabre is also to be avoided!

When you are seated at the table, it is better to be sitting upright and using your back muscles to support your body. You should not be slouching all over the table or chair – that sends out a message that you're being disrespectful to those around you and especially to the person who has presented the meal. Leaning on elbows is another no-no, so I used to say, "Wrists," to my kids, so they would put their wrists on the table for extra support instead of their elbows. Kneeling or sitting with legs and feet on the chair or table are not good either. If your pre-teen is too small to reach the table, put him on a couple of cushions or a booster seat.

Many of us eat our food too quickly and without much actual appreciation for the subtle flavours we taste. Initially, when our son joined the Army, he had very short and irregular meal times and had to rush, but as civilians, we should be making the time to sit, relax and enjoy every meal we eat. This reduces stress to the body and mind, and helps us live better.

When your child has finished his meal and he wishes to leave before everyone else has finished, he needs to ask if he may leave the table and wait for your reply. Usually there is no need to detain him, but if you have an announcement to make or anything special to do, then he should be polite and wait until you're ready. There is a pecking order in the household and the children need to learn that they are respected as part of the household, but they are not at the top of it. When they leave the table, everyone should push their chairs in neatly under the table and take their dirty dishes over to the sink. If washing the dishes is one of their daily tasks, then they should begin the washing process.

Other mannerisms your child may need to refine include interrupting a conversation between two adults. The pre-teen will often participate and engage in other people's discussions, but this is something he needs to learn is not acceptable in all cases. It is pretty cute while he is a baby and a toddler; learning how to speak the language. But once he has a good grasp of it, he needs to learn to say *Excuse me* and wait for a positive response from the people already in discussion. He may then say what he wants to say. This is basic respect for others and if he does this, other people are more likely to make the time to listen to him.

Teach your child about sharing and responsibility

During this time, your little pre-teen needs to learn that he is not the focal point of the family as he once was as a baby and toddler. He is still a vital part of the family, but things are starting to fall into some perspective. He is capable of doing many things on his own and his independence is increasing with every year of his development.

At this time, your child may have younger siblings or pets to consider. He needs to learn the basics of sharing and responsibility. His much-loved toys will be sought after by any younger siblings, so he needs to learn that they can have them for a while and then give them back to him when they've finished playing with them. Some of his toys will be inappropriate for younger children because they have been designed for an older age group, so he needs to make sure they are not left in reach of the curious toddler, who can often destroy something in an instant. That is a hard lesson to learn, so explain to him about the consequences of leaving precious things lying around before he loses something of real value. Remember, it doesn't necessarily need to be valuable, just a precious object to your child.

Your child should be given simple tasks to do on a daily or weekly basis, such as drying the dishes or unstacking the dishwasher, feeding the family pet, making his bed, and tidying his room and clothes. He is learning many things, and the sense of belonging as an integral part of the family is very important. He feels trusted and relied upon to do jobs that mum and dad really appreciate because they're tasks that need to be done to help with the home maintenance. His sense of responsibility increases and he starts to learn about appreciation of things and how to look after them.

One of the best things we found to keep the floors a little cleaner was to take off all footwear and leave it at the door. I printed out a sign, laminated it, and stuck it next to the door so that all visitors understood this was one of our house rules.

The older kids helped the younger ones take off their shoes before coming inside. The great thing about it was they also helped the younger ones put their shoes on when they were leaving to go anywhere, too.

The *Wendy Knot*

One of the neatest things to teach your kids is what I call the *Wendy Knot* – in honour of my friend who taught me how to do it. It is guaranteed *not* to come undone until you want it to, so no more tripping over sloppy shoe laces!

It is a double knot that can be untied as easily as a normal Bow knot; it just needs a bit more of a tug. If you teach your kids how to do it, then they can use it all their lives whenever they tie runners or laced shoes that they don't want to come undone at an inopportune moment.

You start the knot the same way as you would a normal Bow knot, but when you have curled one loop through under the other one, just repeat the same process so you have looped it around two times. Pull it tight and even up the lace ends and there you have it – the *Wendy Knot*!

TIP FOR LEFT-HANDED CHILDREN

If you are a right-handed person and you have a left-handed child (or vice versa), one way to teach him how to tie his shoe laces is to face him and ask him to copy your actions as if he is mirroring you. Then you can do it naturally without confusing yourself and him!

Your pre-teen is growing in his body and also in his perceptual ability. He is learning to recognise that things aren't always black and white, but grey areas are beginning to appear. He is learning that sometimes people can be nice, and other times they might be in a bad mood. He might think he is the cause of the bad mood, but unless he has actually done something to warrant the blame, he should realise that it's nothing to do with him. People can change their behaviour for any number of reasons, and he may need to learn to cope with that, especially if he lives in the same household as that person. Giving them time and space, and letting them work it out may be the best method to clear the air. If it cannot be resolved easily, however, a third party may need to intervene to help resolve any outstanding issues. Above all, the safety and well-being of your pre-teen and any siblings is paramount.

Encourage, encourage, encourage

During the pre-teen years, your child will attempt many things and make many mistakes. Your job is to let him feel a sense of discouragement when he fails, but then encourage him to have another go. Continually encourage him and tell him that failure is only a part of the process of learning. Most of us learn our lessons better and remember them for longer when we have made a mistake first. Theoretical lessons can help ward off many potential mistakes, but those learned by the *School of Hard Knocks* usually stick with you for life.

Persistence will bring success. When persistence is combined with some knowledge, then success should come a little faster. It's not a guarantee because everyone takes a different route to find their path to success, but if you keep doing what needs to be done, it will happen.

Success can be different for each of us and when we examine the motivation for most actions in life, the underlying desire is to be happy.

> FINDING HAPPINESS WILL BRING YOU SUCCESS,
> BUT BEING SUCCESSFUL WON'T NECESSARILY BRING YOU HAPPINESS.

13

Teenager Basics

Teenagers can be both kids and adults
and change in an instant.

Instructions:

1. Read the Introduction.
2. Patience really is a virtue.
3. Relinquish the desire to *control.*
4. Organised physical activity is a must.
5. Life goals keep the direction focussed.
6. Teenagers grow before your eyes.
7. Teenage girls need patience and personal space.
8. Teenage boys need food and a physical outlet.
9. Pre-marital sex is common.
10. Underage drinking must be avoided.
11. Give your kids advanced driver training.
12. It's *never* too late.
13. Practice *unconditional* love.

Your child has turned thirteen and sooner or later you may find it hard to recognise him anymore. This is most easily observed at the physical level, but is present at the emotional and mental level as well. His sleeping patterns extend and he needs around 10 hours of sleep a night. If he doesn't have this, then he may appear to be in a constant state of dullness and stupor. His reactions may be slow and clumsy, at least until after he has eaten, which tends to be anything that happens to be in the pantry or fridge at the time. Both boys and girls increase their food intake, so it is wise to keep fresh and raw foods around; not too many snacks or highly processed foods, as they will be eaten first and regretted later.

Not only does he start to change the style of clothes he wears, but his attitude undergoes a make-over, too. What might start out as a minor disagreement can escalate into a major argument with all the frills – yelling, tears, hurtful comments, 'he said – she said', 'you said – I said', stomping away, and slamming doors. When you have had a moment or two to calm down and reflect on what has just happened it isn't unusual for a parent to quizzically ask, *What just happened here?* The response you might get is about as realistic as, *An* alien *just possessed my kid!*

Living with one or more teenagers in the house is really quite simple; about as simple as dropping a box of toothpicks and having then all fall in line! Not very likely, and not likely to happen to you if it does. Having said that, there are times when your teenager will surprise you with his wisdom, and his love. You just have to last the distance. By the time he reaches 18 or 19, he has usually started to settle down and can claim to be more *human* again.

Patience really is a virtue

At this time of your child's development, it really helps to have an abundance of patience. Now there are physiological elements coming into play, as well as the usual elements of respect conflicts, feelings of insufficiency and insecurity, and a myriad of others that I'm sure we could all relate to as we were growing up. In a word – puberty! It hits, and the child who we know and adore may start behaving in ways that have no logic or reason. It affects each child differently and to a lesser or greater extent, but it does have an effect on each child.

Just keep reminding yourself, *It's the hormones. It's only the hormones!* Think of it as a daily mantra, if you like. Do whatever it takes to keep yourself calm and under true self-control, as opposed to the pretend one, where we act calm and collected, but are seething underneath, ready to explode at any second! When I would start to feel the blood boiling in my neck, that's when I knew it was time to escape and go away – outside, anywhere – before something regretful would happen. Big, deep breaths; closed, relaxing eyes, smiling at some distant, humorous thought; and a neck massage always brought me back to a state of relative peace – the neck massage was the *dream* I used to have while trying to relax. Unfortunately, no one was around to do the massage when I needed it!

One of my sons became extremely conscious of his skin and the acne on it. I'm not sure whether his growing obsession made it worse, but he became so unhappy about it, that some mornings he flatly refused to go to school. You can imagine what went on – firstly, the rationalising, then the pleading, and finally, the ordering – none of which worked.

In the end, we realised that it was far less traumatic just to let him stay at home and work it out for himself. He may have missed a few more days at school than his mates, but it didn't really affect his academic scoring.

Relinquish the desire to *control*

Your kids are starting to need some space from mum and dad. If you are still *seen* to be controlling them in some way – whether this is true, is irrelevant – then this can cause more issues as time progresses. The *perception* which your teenager has of a situation is all that matters to him and you need to understand and respect this state. You don't have to agree with it, but you need to respect the fact that your teenager has a right to his opinion.

If he still has a high degree of trust in you, then the inevitable disagreements will be less energetic and may be put off for some time. But, if he has lost trust in you, he will put up an emotional barrier and start to doubt your opinion. Eventually, he may even stop listening to you and walk away, or turn up the volume on his music and ignore you completely. The loss of *trust* leads to this loss of *respect* and it has usually been caused by some of your more careless choices over the years, such as making fun of him a bit too much while he was younger, or embarrassing him in public, or just not considering his opinions as valid even if they may have been a bit naive. These are some of the more subtle mistakes you may have made to produce this result.

There are more serious and obvious actions, such as physical or verbal abuse, that can lead to a child becoming secretive, withdrawn, and over-sensitive. This type of abusive behaviour may begin as something relatively small – a slap across the face, or a swear word spat out in frustration and anger – but it can develop into something much more destructive and lead you to a very unhappy and lonely place.

As the adult of the relationship, you need to show your *'apprentice adult'* (your teenager) the more mature approach to conflict resolution and problem solving. Factual, unemotional, and respectful communication should be established in all situations, with all parties given a chance to speak and give their version of the event. Remember that everyone has a unique viewpoint, and each is equally valid. When you have all the details before you, the conclusions that should be drawn usually become obvious to those who are present and behaving reasonably.

Sometimes, there may be an underlying medical issue, especially if a parent feels an excessive need to be in control all the time. This may occur in situations where the parent is suffering from Obsessive Compulsive Disorder (OCD) – often characterised by the need to have everything in order, from the tins in the pantry, to the shoes on the porch, or the way the curtain falls from the railing.

The mother mentioned in the chapter *Prevention is Better than Cure* was suffering from OCD, but it was undiagnosed and untreated. Her family loved her and made up excuses for her behaviour – the favourite excuse was that her father had become violent after he came back from the war and he often became very physical with the family members.

This mother dominated the home environment. Not only did she antiseptically clean the house, but no one was allowed to touch the fridge, get their own food, or ask for the salt and pepper, unless she had first placed it on the table. If she felt like it wasn't needed, then NO ONE needed it. If you asked for it, then you effectively insulted her. Nothing in the house was to be done without her permission. When she became upset (often), she would use the silent treatment as a punishment for the family, so no one really knew what was wrong, what had upset her, or what could be done to resolve the situation.

You can imagine how destructive this type of environment was for her young children. They grew up walking on 'egg-shells', having to tip-toe around the house; watching every word that was said or action that was done in case it was perceived incorrectly and upset her. These children grew up feeling emotionally incapacitated because their lives were spent revolving around someone else to help her feel valued, while they were missing out on finding out about themselves and what they wanted out of life.

The parents of these children loved them dearly, but because of their ignorance and denial of the problem, they were unable to value their own children properly, so they grew up with resentments and emotional scarring.

What saved these children was organised sport. They started a sport to help with the younger child's asthma and this finally gave both children a worthy goal upon which to focus. The parents were involved as administrators and helpers, so the entire family participated. Life improved somewhat, and the kids became champions.

The behaviour of an adult shouldn't be ignored no matter what the excuse. When a person becomes an adult, he or she has a simple choice: to behave properly and fairly, or not. If the person cannot make that choice freely, then they need help and a doctor or recognised health practitioner should be consulted about the issue.

Organised physical activity is a must

During the teenage years, both girls and boys need to participate in some *organised* physical exercise. By organised, I mean an activity that is coordinated, regular, and preferably conducted by someone *other* than yourself or your partner. Your child is becoming an adult and needs to do more and more activities where he makes the decisions that affect him. School sport is an excellent way to do this because your teenager is still in a relatively safe environment where he is getting the benefits of physical exercise and learning to socialise in a constructive way with like-minded people. He is also taking instruction from another person who is not his parent or regular teacher and this can provide him with another role model in his life. This is important as it can act as a guide for his choice of friends in the future.

Team sports, such as football (any code) or basketball, or more individual pursuits, like the martial arts (any discipline), swimming, gymnastics or dance, are excellent activities. These days, the list is almost endless, so ensure your teenager chooses carefully so he isn't changing activities too often. Obviously, if your teenager starts something that he doesn't want to continue after three months, then change to something else. There is no point in forcing him to do something he just doesn't like. Listen to him and take notice of the messages he is telling you – whether directly or more subtly – a high absentee rate indicates quite clearly that the child or teenager is not interested in the activity.

When we all started Taekwondo, our ages were 9, 11, 13, 15, and 44. We had a great time because the style we chose involved *controlled contact*, so we were able to learn the techniques and patterns without suffering injuries – except for the odd bruise or two!

We continued with it for a number of years because it was something we could all do and enjoy. After the three eldest attained their Black Belt qualifications they decided to try other things. My youngest had already left the sport to pursue other sporting interests and that was absolutely fine. I was happy as long as they were involved in some form of sporting pursuit.

For those of you who think age is a barrier, at the time of writing, I am still practising and enjoying the art of Taekwondo. I have had my 2nd Degree Black Belt for over 3 years and have turned 53 this year. If you have a goal, then go for it. No excuses!

When you choose to participate in the activities of your teenager, you are sending him the message that he is important to you, that you are very interested in what he likes, and that you want to be a part of his life. When you participate as an equal – a player, not an organiser – you are saying to him that you don't want to control his life; you want to co-exist. If you only participate as a bystander, and merely become a spectator of his life, then you may be doing yourself a disservice and could become a slave to his desires. Yes, he appreciates you being there, and dropping him off and picking him up, but in reality, no more than a taxi service. This may lead to resentment, which will be covered later.

If you are unable to do more than observe, whether through physical incapacity or otherwise, you can still become involved through your observations. Be another set of eyes for him and on the way home discuss the game or the state of play. Engage his impressions about how it went and if he felt he played well or how others performed. You may become his personal coach, but be careful you don't become over-committed to his success. Many parents overdo the coaching part and end up alienating their child because they push him further than he wishes to go. His expectations become overshadowed by the parent's expectations and suddenly the success of the child is now a reflection of the success of the parent. The whole point of the exercise is lost.

If your current lifestyle, physical state, or work commitments do not allow you the freedom to participate with your teenager's activities, then you need to seriously consider what you can change about *your* life to make it happen. Ultimately, the choice is up to you, but you should at least consider the consequences of your actions to their fullest extent, including your relationship with your teenager. It's all a matter of priorities. What are yours?

Once he has grown up and left home, you can devote your time to whatever you like. But, there is no second chance or extra time while your kids are young and still at home with you. Don't waste this time.

Life goals keep the direction focussed

Kids who have a clear goal in life are generally better focussed at school and in their normal daily activities. The age at which a child decides what they would like as their life career varies greatly, but it appears to be an advantage to know, or at least have a good idea, by the time he reaches 15 or 16 years old. If he doesn't know at this age, that's still OK, but there is just more uncertainty in his life and he can be more easily distracted by other things, such as computer games or hanging out with his friends. If he doesn't have a clear goal, in our society, he needs to be aware of the importance of having a capacity to earn a living. As parents, you need to encourage all your teenagers to get casual jobs where they can learn new skills and feel the improvement in self-esteem that comes with earning some money. They are also really happy with the increased spending power their new activity can provide.

This is an ideal time to introduce the concept of *wealth* and its creation in your teenager's life. An excellent book to give to or read with your teenager is *The Richest Man in Babylon*.[56] It introduces the concept of always saving the first 10% of your earnings (whatever they are) for wealth creation and putting it into a secure account, such as a savings or term deposit account with a reputable bank or financial institution. The remaining 90% needs to be divided up as 70% for basic living expenses and 20% to pay back any existing debt. Hopefully, your teenager doesn't yet have any debt accrued, so the 20% can be put into the wealth fund along with the 10%. This instils a mindset of saving and living within ones means, as opposed to the credit society, where people are encouraged to spend more than they earn and accrue massive amounts of debt with little hope of repaying it back. This earning and savings mindset will not only help your teenager to start his own wealth creation program, but will encourage him to stay focussed and continue to follow this pattern throughout his life no matter what his career.

Teenagers grow before your eyes

The body of a teenager normally goes through major changes. If you stare at him long enough, you can almost *see* him growing! He will often appear to spring up overnight and friends or relatives who haven't seen him for a month or so will notice a dramatic increase in height and sometimes body mass. The increase in height can often precede a period of awkwardness or apparent clumsiness and this can largely be due to the body's inability to realign and balance itself quickly enough as it attempts to cope with the body's own growth spurt. I'm sure many of us have heard of expressions like *the gangly lad*, which refers to the teenage boy whose long bones (arms and

---

[56]   Clason, George S, *The Richest Man in Babylon*, 1955.

legs) are stretching out rapidly, making him appear a little out of proportion with the rest of his body.

> My husband visits an osteopath regularly to help him maintain his spinal flexibility due to an old injury. We used to take the kids along every six months or so, just to have a check up, or if they had fallen off the top bunk or a swing.
>
> At one of these sessions, the osteopath noticed one of our sons had one leg shorter than the other. This could have become a major problem because the longer leg would have had increased pressure upon it, thereby encouraging it to grow even faster than the shorter one. The pressure on the leg's bony growth plates (epiphysial cells) encourages them to lay down more cells and hence the growth is more at that point.
>
> Because our son was still growing, we were able to rectify the problem using a heel wedge that had to be worn inside his shoe. This wedge provided the needed pressure on his shorter leg, thereby allowing it to grow more and catch up with the other one over time.

The obvious physical growth can obscure a more subtle emotional and mental development that is largely controlled by the body's changing hormonal levels. If these levels become a little unbalanced, they may help to produce the *Alien Possession* effect most parents of teenagers have experienced.

Teenage girls need patience and personal space

Your teenage daughter needs patience from you and the rest of the family as she struggles with issues like body image; lack of confidence; insecurity among peers; competition within the family; and what she will do when she leaves school, to name just a few. She may not appear to be concerned about some or any of these things, but if you observe long enough, you can see traces of them, even among the most confident teenager. A simple question is to ask her what she sees when she looks in the mirror, or even if she *can* look in a mirror. Many teenagers are too insecure to even face themselves apart from a brief, cursory glance.

Show her patience, understanding, and love, especially when she feels and acts troubled. Sometimes she doesn't even know why she is behaving in an angry or spiteful way. She does love you, even when she is angry with you, but she can't always help her frustration with the imbalance of chemicals flowing through her body. It helps you to remember that and keep calm.

However, if you feel the level of respect is being lowered too much, and basic manners are being ignored, remind her of this as gently as you can. Without anger in your voice, just let her know that you are feeling that her behaviour is becoming disrespectful and that it needs to change. Then leave it at that and walk away. This gives her time to consider your words, take on their meaning and, hopefully, adjust her behaviour without being told any further. Teenagers hate to be told, so no nagging!

If you focus on her *behaviour* being unacceptable, and not *her* being so, that subtle difference is telling her that you still love her for what she is, but you don't like the things she might be saying or doing at this time.

> DON'T BREAK THE SPIRIT,
> TREAT THE BEHAVIOUR, NOT THE PERSON.

Teenage girls often seem to become obsessed with their appearance and their relative status within their peer group. They may start to wear make-up and tend to take a great deal of trouble dressing for an outing – even if the result doesn't necessarily look like it. They also may become very shy about their bodies (except with their trusted friends) and need their own personal space just to do things and think about things without being interrupted by siblings or other family members. Their privacy is important and even though you might think there is no need for them to feel embarrassed, they do, and that should be respected.

I remember when my mum took me to buy my first bra. I did not want her in the dressing cubicle with me and I felt really embarrassed about asking her to leave. She did, but only after expressing her disbelief at me: *Why do I need to leave? We're all female!* This made me feel silly and that my viewpoint was insignificant.

She was probably right at some level, but her reaction wasn't what I needed at that age. Years later, I couldn't have cared less who came in with me – as long as she was female or one of my own kids!

As a teenager myself, I used to think that some of the girls were going a bit silly, but then I had my own issues, and as a nerdy-tom-boy type, I preferred to read books at lunchtime or play sport, than whisper secrets and giggle about boys. They were my soccer-choc and footy buddies and certainly not an object of desire (whatever *that* was) – yuck! Okay, I was a late developer, so what?

The imbalance of hormones in girls may declare itself as overly flirtatious or permissive behaviour. The body is sending messages to the brain saying that it is ready for procreation, and in some cultures this is perfectly acceptable. But in the Western civilisation and society, we seek to suppress and frown upon this behaviour – at least at the superficial level.

Recent psychological studies on the early onset of puberty in girls aged between 6 – 8 years of age indicated that the absence of a biological father in families with a higher income had more of an impact than body mass index or the presence of other males in the household.[57]

Other studies of young girls living with a male parent (or equivalent) who was not their biological father showed a marked increase in flirtatious behaviour directed towards him. This could possibly be attributed to an instinctual desire to procreate with a mate who has a different gene pool.

The result of these studies may indicate a simple case of survival of the fittest, and not necessarily an issue with a wanton girl being intentionally destructive to herself, to her mother, or to her mother's partner.

Your daughter needs to know about her bodily changes over this time and more importantly, how to cope with them. The current education system does cover much of the physical aspects of menarche[58], but some things only a mother can pass on, such as her own experiences with it and how it affects her. Your daughter will probably have a similar experience, so if, for example, you have suffered bad menstrual cramps, then your daughter may suffer a similar condition. It would be prudent and compassionate to talk to her about it and about pain relief methods you may have found useful. Don't be embarrassed to talk about these things; they are a natural occurrence and should be discussed openly, honestly, and in private. The last thing your pubescent daughter wants is a nosey younger brother asking awkward

---

[57] Deardorff, J., et al. *Father Absence, Body Mass Index, and Pubertal Timing in Girls: Differential Effects by Family Income and Ethnicity.* Journal of Adolescent Health, 2011 May, **48**(5): 441-447.

[58] The onset of menstruation.

questions. The respect you show to your daughter at this time will be returned in kind, and she will know she can talk to you about anything without the fear of ridicule or embarrassment. If either of you have any concerns, then you can discuss them with your family doctor in confidence.

Prepare your daughter for the admiring attentions of young men as she grows older. It is flattering for her to think she can inspire admiration in someone else not attached to the family. Let her know she is worthy of it, but does not have to respond in kind. Many, if not all, of us have felt the pangs of a little infatuation or crush on someone around us; often towards a teacher or older mentor. Most of us are too embarrassed to tell anyone about it, so the crush stays within our hearts and passes over time without ever seeing the light of day.

Sometimes, your daughter might not like the person who admires her. If this is so, remind her to be aware of this person's feelings and how fragile they are at this time. She needs to watch her behaviour to ensure she is not encouraging him inadvertently; the balance between being considerate and letting him down gently, and him thinking she is merely toying with him so he should keep trying, can be quite difficult to find. In the end, it may be necessary to bluntly tell him to go away and to leave her alone.

On the other hand, if your daughter likes the person who admires her, she needs to be reminded to move along at a slow pace. There are many steps along the way to romance and each should be enjoyed for the delight, or otherwise, it might bring. If the relationship is merely an infatuation, these simple, preliminary steps will watch it pass without much effort or pain. If there is more affection on both sides, then taking things carefully will help it to build into something very special. From the first glance and embarrassed smile that locked eyes can create, through to holding hands, and that first kiss; each needs to be savoured, like a good wine or a favourite dish. It should be something that is very private and special; not to be broadcast to the masses like a conquest or award. This is distasteful and offensive, and it demeans the relationship and both participants. The notion that a relationship – any relationship – should head towards a sexual encounter is false. This is something reserved for a special person and not to be offered around like lollies.

Tell your daughter that it is fairly easy for a man to trick a girl into doing something (sexually) that she may regret for many years to come. A little flattery to an unwitting teenager will break down many defences. Dorothy

Rowe, a leading clinical psychologist, has stated that *a standing cock has no conscience.* [59]

Certainly, no one intends for their daughter to be promiscuous, so you need to educate your daughter on the virtues of *mateship love,*[60] which is the blending and merging of love and sex. This is closer to *true* love, if you like, because it is based on an affectionate and respectful understanding between two people that has lasted a period of time spanning months or even years, rather than hours. The motivation for the event should never be based on attention-getting or power-seeking, nor as a poor substitute for unrequited love.

Stick by your teenage daughter and believe in her and her abilities; educate her as fully as possible so she has the ability to make informed choices in her life; encourage her to do what feels right for her; and then expect her to do so. And always welcome her into your heart; a sincere and loving hug can cure many ills.

BEAUTY TIPS FOR TEENAGE GIRLS

The following tips are fairly general and are a guide only.

BODY: Everybody is slightly different, but if you eat correctly, drink plenty of water, and exercise regularly (including flexibility and stretching activities), you should be able to maintain a healthy body weight.

If you can get out in the sun without any sunscreens for 15-20 minutes every day between 0800 and 0900, that is ideal because you will not get burnt, and your body will make Vitamin D. This will ward off a myriad of diseases later in life, especially during pregnancy and senescence (old age).

Be aware that some things, like taking the contraceptive pill and having emotional issues in your life, can predispose you to weight gain, whether through holding fluids, or eating more sweet foods. If you confront your issues, the short term pain will always be offset by the longer term benefits.

SKIN: Your skin is an organ of your body. If you like, it is a mirror of what is going on inside your body and how your other organs are fairing. To keep it clear and glowing, you need to look after your whole body through proper eating, drinking plenty of water, exercising regularly, getting some morning sun at least weekly, and getting plenty of rest.

---

[59]   Rowe, D. *Why We Lie: The Source of Our Disasters*, 2010.
[60]   Rikard-Bell, R. *Loving Sex: Happiness in Mateship*, 1990, pg 5.

FACE: Every girl needs to be told that she is beautiful – when she starts to believe it, she shines. The old adage – *beauty is only skin deep* – is only true at the superficial level. Real beauty stems from the heart and is more a factor of the love and respect she shares with others.

Having said the above, from about the age of 15, teenage girls should start to follow a skin care regimen; or earlier if they have already started using make-up. Pick a good cleanser and moisturiser and use it at least once a day, preferably at night to remove the dirt and any make-up from the day. I use organic products as much as possible, and use fresh water as a toner. The moisturiser should not be heavy on your skin and apply it to dampened skin so it spreads easily, evenly, and lightly. The effects of gravity take their toll over time, so use light upward strokes on your face and neck using your ring fingers because they have a lighter touch. Be very gentle with the skin around your eyes – the muscles underneath are like fine cobwebs – so pat them lightly, rather than drag across them. This helps avoid premature baggy eyes in later years.

MAKE-UP: This is a personal choice, but remember that the goal for make-up artists for celebrities is to make it look like they're *not* wearing make-up! The old adage: *Less is best* is true for make-up, especially for young people. Sure, if you want to dress up for a party, go for it, but in your daily activities, leave your skin able to breathe, and learn to love your own face for its simple beauty. Also, if you wear foundation, make sure you smooth it in under your chin (using a soft latex sponge), so it doesn't have a distinct cut-off line around your jaw; a really bad look. And, clean it all off at the end of the day so your skin's pores can breathe overnight.

HAIR: Hair is composed of a protein called keratin. It is the same stuff of which your nails are made. The sebaceous glands at the base of the hair shaft secrete sebum, which is an oil that keeps the hair shaft pliable, soft, and shiny. Washing your hair too frequently can remove the sebum and make your hair dry and brittle. Conditioners can be used to maintain a soft texture, but choose one that doesn't make your hair too oily too quickly, because then you will be tempted to wash your hair too often. Rinse your hair with cool water as this tends to close the hair shaft and make it smoother, silkier, and easier to manage.

Heat denatures (destroys) proteins and that is what it will do to your hair, so use heated appliances on your hair with great care. Keep their use infrequent or consider not using them at all. I don't blow dry my hair, nor use straighteners nor curling wands; I prefer to keep my hair intact.

Dying your hair should also be done with care; over-bleaching will eventually destroy the hair follicle and hence the quality of your hair. Again, it's a matter of priorities and your personal sense of style and fashion. Keep these destructive processes to a minimum, especially as a young person.

NAILS: Trim or file your nails regularly to keep them healthy. File them in one-way only – usually from the outside to the mid point – as this helps to prevent the nail from splitting. After you have moisturised your face and hands, remember to gently push back the cuticle of each nail to keep them pliable. Consider buffing your nails regularly to a shine, rather than using harsh nail polishes. The chemicals are very strong and overpowering, so always apply them in a well-ventilated area to avoid getting headaches.

Teenage boys need food and a physical outlet

Teenage boys are more basic and often much less mature than their female counterparts. Their main focus appears to be foraging for food. The hunter awakens and the first thing they seem to do when they wake up or come home is check out the fridge. Anything that takes their fancy tends to be seen as prey. If you're lucky, they might ask you if they can eat it, but it's usually prudent to stick a note on it if you need it for later. These boys tend to live by the *It's easier to ask for forgiveness, than permission* principle. So be prepared; have a spare loaf of bread around, a kilo of cheese, and about 3 litres of milk as a baseline. And that's just for one day, especially if they are doing some decent exercise or sporting activities!

Like most of us, teenage boys need to feel part of a team and to have a vital role in that team, even if it's only small. That's why organised sporting activities are an excellent outlet for all that pent-up testosterone.

My boys loved all types of physical exercise and over the years had a go at football, rock climbing, running, athletics, kick boxing, cycling taekwondo, and kung fu.

What I was most impressed about was their willingness to try any activity – and sometimes stretch that to volunteering a parent. I remember one time we were travelling up to the Brisbane Cricket Ground (the Gabba) in a bus full of little Auskick kids from school.

The Sports Teacher asked, "Who know the rules of AFL?" My adorable son proudly said, "My mum does!" I was promptly handed the umpire's whistle and sports top and told, "You're going to referee the match!" That was a mild shock, but what was more amazing was going out onto that huge arena's grassy playing field at the half-time break of the real AFL match that was being played, and umpire the kids' game right in front of the Member's Stand! Talk about pressure!

Your teenage boy may need to be pushed a bit, especially in the later years, and that can be hard for some mothers who still think of him as their darling baby. Nothing will change that, especially when he persists in asking you to validate his existence: *Do you still love me, Mummy?* In spite of an impulse to say to the contrary, just to shock him, I decided not to, because I didn't want to plant any seeds of insecurity in his still young and impressionable mind.

Like all teenagers, boys need to learn life skills, such as how to tidy their own room, put on a load of washing, do the dishes, cook a meal, and take out the garbage. Hopefully, many of these skills have already been taught in the pre-teen or early teenage years because it is much easier to do it at that time. It gets harder as he ages and becomes more self-focussed. Persist with him, and explain about the consequences of his actions. Tell him your intentions and your reasoning and then give him some simple goals to do in a specific time-frame.

For example, at the end of each week, you'd like him to put all his dirty clothes in the laundry. And that's it. Not too difficult a task; well within the normal teenage boy's list of accomplishments, and at least it's something that you don't have to do anymore.

After a period of time, when the task has become commonplace and you don't have to remind him anymore, you can add another simple task to the list.

For example, every day, please separate the rubbish from the recyclables in your room. Here are two bins; put the recyclables, such as paper, aluminium cans, aerosols, glass containers, in the one marked *Recyclables* and the rest can go in the one marked *Rubbish*. On the day before rubbish collection day, please empty your bins into the appropriate wheelie bins. Here are the plastic bags, or newspaper, to line your rubbish bin. Then you can wrap up your rubbish before you throw it out. Leave the recyclables separate and unwrapped so the workers at the recycling factory can easily sort each item. As simple as these tasks are, they are giving your teenager something else to think about and to do on a daily or weekly basis.

If your teenage boy hasn't yet found a career path, have patience with him and help him find a casual job. This will usually help him decide what he doesn't like, as well as top up his bank account. It might not be a burning passion for him, but he should be encouraged to give it a go for at least six months to one year. That's the only way he'll know if he loves it, or hates it. If he sticks with it for that period of time, he also learns about concentrated effort and persistence, which are more life skills. The time is never wasted even if he chooses to move away from it. When he has decided on a clear direction to go, he will focus on it and change any habits that are counter-productive to that goal.

When my son decided to join the Army he was 16 but was encouraged by the Army recruiters to finish his final Year 12 and join up after he turned 18 years of age. He did so, and after he joined the army and passed his recruitment training period, we were so proud to see him marching around the parade ground with his mates. It was a defining moment in all of our lives.

His brother then decided to join the army as well. He made it down to the Army Recruitment Training Base, but after three weeks, decided it wasn't for him and handed in his resignation papers. They kept him there for another three weeks, all the while telling him how he would be great in the army, but to no avail.

After he came home, his attitude had changed enough that he started hospital-cornering his bed, then he cleaned out his cupboards and everything left was folded up into neat little parcels of about 25cm x 10cm. The biggest advantage we found was his changed attitude towards the online computer-based games with which he had become obsessed. He came home and played for far less time than he devoted to his Kung Fu training, and his playing time has continued to decrease considerably more since then.

I realised then that Army recruitment training for at least six weeks should be mandatory for all young men who have no clear direction in life. An absolute winner!

Every teenage boy needs to respect the girls around him, especially the ones close to his own age. He needs to understand that some of them may flirt with him and try to get his attention, but he should be polite to them, and leave them alone. These girls may draw him into a relationship that means trouble. As with teenage girls, the boys need tutoring on mateship love,[61] and that they are on the whole too young and immature to be feeding their desires with just anyone who offers it. She may have her reasons, but it is disrespectful to perform an act without any feelings of attachment and love. He is worth more than that, and the young lady should be told that too.

The extent of sexual arousal your son may or may not feel can vary dramatically, but is probably attributable to a combination of factors like genetics, learned behaviour, personal self-esteem, and self-confidence. He may become aroused by simply watching a pretty girl walk along the street, or it may take much closer personal contact to achieve anything like an erection. Either way, he needs to understand what is expected of him should he choose to enter into a relationship with another person.

A relationship can and often does occur in the teenage years; students from the same school will often form an alliance of some sort, but while they are under the legal age, taking the relationship to a sexual level is completely irresponsible. There is a reason for the minimum age, so use it as a minimum standard. If your son likes the person who admires him, he needs to be reminded to move along at a slow pace. There are many steps along the way to romance and each should be enjoyed for the delight, or otherwise, it might bring. If the relationship is merely an infatuation, these simple, preliminary steps will watch it pass without much effort or pain. If there is more affection on both sides, then taking things carefully will help it to build into something very special. From the first glance and embarrassed smile that locked eyes can create, through to holding hands, and that first kiss; each needs to be savoured, like a good wine or a favourite dish. It should be something that is very private and special. The notion that a relationship − any relationship − should head towards a sexual encounter is false. This is something reserved for a special person and them alone. When a sexual act does occur, ensure your son is aware of how to use a condom correctly. The risks are too great, and it's his responsibility to put it on properly. If you find it hard to talk

---

[61]   Mateship Love: The blending and merging of love and sex.
   Rikard-Bell, R. *Loving Sex: Happiness in Mateship*, 1990, pg 5.

with your son about these issues, seek help from your family GP. He will tell him the plain facts without judgement or recrimination, so your son can be informed without feeling guilty or shameful.

HYGIENE TIPS FOR TEENAGE BOYS

The following tips are fairly general and are a guide only.

BODY: Boys need to wash their bodies at least once a day, and always at night before they go to bed to ensure all the dirt and sweat of the day has been washed away.

Everybody is slightly different, but if you eat correctly, drink plenty of water, and exercise regularly (including flexibility, strength, and stretching activities), you should be able to maintain a healthy body weight.

Strength or weight exercises should be started using the body's own weight and gradually increasing the number of repetitions, such as with chin ups or push ups. After 16 or 17 years, a regimen of light weights and multiple repetitions may be started. Heavier weights should only be applied gradually and after the long bones have finished their major growth spurt – any time after 18 to 21+ years old. Flexibility exercises should always be combined with weight training so that the full range of body movements is not compromised. Muscle bound males are highly inflexible and that can be a problem for the healthy body, especially later in life.

Sweating is the body's natural air conditioning system. In my opinion, blocking it up with an antiperspirant is going against nature, so choose deodorants that have natural ingredients and do not contain aluminium.[62] The cause of smelly underarms, especially after heavy labour or vigorous exercise, is a by-product of bacterial growth in the hair follicles and sweat glands of the skin. One of the most effective ways I found to avoid this it to soak a cotton ball in Eucalyptus Oil or Tea Tree Oil and rub it all over your arm pit. This helps to remove dead skin cells, stagnant sebum deposits, and kills the bacteria. You might smell like a tree for a couple of days, but then you only need to use a milder deodorant afterwards and the effect can last for weeks, depending upon your personal hygiene habits.

---

[62] Exley, C. *Does antiperspirant use increase the risk of aluminium-related disease, including Alzheimer's disease?* Molecular Medicine Today, Mar 1998, pg 107-9.

If you can get out in the sun without any sunscreens for 15-20 minutes every day between 0800 and 0900, that is ideal because you will not get burnt, and your body will make Vitamin D. This will help ward off many diseases in life, such as rickets and osteoporosis.[63]

Sometimes emotional issues in your life can predispose you to weight gain or skin eruptions. If you confront your issues, the short term pain will always be offset by the longer term benefits.

SKIN: Your skin is an organ of your body. If you like, it is a mirror of what is going on inside your body and how your other organs are fairing. To keep it clear and glowing, you need to look after your whole body through proper eating, drinking plenty of water, exercising regularly, getting some morning sun at least weekly, reducing the toxins put into your body (through fast foods and soft drinks), and getting plenty of rest.

FACE: A confident teenager does not concern himself about small eruptions on his face. I am convinced the emotional trauma can lead to recurring problems because of the obsessive nature of some personality types. The more he thinks about it, the worse it becomes, no matter what he does. If he starts to have real problems with acne, then consult your GP. Sometimes home remedies can help, such as drinking a glass of freshly squeezed lemon juice before each meal.

HAIR: Hair is composed of a protein called keratin. It is the same stuff of which your nails are made. The sebaceous glands at the base of the hair shaft secrete sebum, which is an oil that keeps the hair shaft pliable, soft, and shiny. Washing your hair too frequently can remove the sebum and make your hair dry and brittle. Conditioners can be used to maintain a soft texture, but choose one that doesn't make your hair too oily too quickly, because then you will be tempted to wash your hair too often.

The use of heated appliances on your hair must be done with great care. Heat denatures (destroys) proteins and that is what it will do to your hair, so make their use infrequent or consider not using them at all. I don't blow dry my hair, I prefer to keep it intact.

Dying your hair should be done with care; over-bleaching will eventually destroy the hair follicle and hence the quality of your hair. It's a matter of priorities and your personal sense of style and fashion. Keep these destructive processes to a minimum, especially as a young person.

---

[63]   http://en.wikipedia.org/wiki/Vitamin_D

> NAILS: Trim or file your nails regularly to keep them healthy. File them in one-way only – usually from the outside to the mid point – as this helps to prevent the nail from splitting. Toe nails should be cut straight across to avoid in-grown toe nails; wear loose socks and well-fitted shoes with plenty of room for growing feet.

Pre-marital sex is common

Like it or not, the ideal of waiting for the marriage night to have your first sexual experience is as outdated as it is improbable. Two generations ago, it was common, but not anymore. Even royal marriages don't have that expectation, and the most recent royal wedding occurred after the couple had known each other for 10 years, some of which time was spent living together.

This subject needs to be discussed with your teenager. Again, it can be as simple or as complicated as you deem necessary and that depends to a very large extent on the baggage you bring to the discussion table. If you bring illogical arguments and guilt to the table, then be prepared for a fight. Teenagers will not, and in their defence, should not have to accept an opinion just because it is their parent's opinion. If you can prove its merit through years of experience and trial, then that is far better than pure conjecture or ignorant words.

The subject itself has always been very touchy because of the myriad of religious, moral, and social opinions that threaten any open discussion about it. If you are from a very religious background, you will have a strong direction to follow and one that makes you comfortable. If so, go down that path. It is clear to you. Just remember to be tolerant of others and their independent opinions. If you are the type of person who fears what the neighbours will say, then you need to stop living in fear; any power they have over you is only in proportion to what you allow them. Don't give it to them.

If we take a step back and look at humanity over the ages, we can see that the social mores and customs of the day have varied widely through the centuries, but have they prevented the instinctual patterns and desires of the people they claim to represent? Not really. The ancient Romans were well-known for their orgies, and through all the ages to today the illegitimate offspring of the kings, prominent people, and even popes of the day, have sometimes made a huge influence on humanity itself. Just look at Leonardo

Da Vinci, one of the most admired and revered people since the 15th Century – genius and illegitimate. Unplanned or unwanted pregnancies have always happened; they have just been covered up, sometimes more successfully than others. Most of the torrid secrets that seek to ruin the reputation of so-called pious families can be attributed in part to some form of sexual deviation, greed or pride. And the fear of discovery binds them all together. Do you want to live that way – with lies, deceit, and secrets eating away at your soul every day?

As a loving and protective parent, you need to understand that no matter how much you think you know your teenager, he or she may be keeping secrets from you. Depending upon your attitude and demeanour, this may be a good idea. If you are of the opinion that it's OK for boys to do this, but not for girls, then you need to rethink that viewpoint. In this case, your daughter should have the option to keep her secrets because she may see it as a safety mechanism:

If Dad or Mum knew I was doing this, they'd kill me!

This might be just an expression, but the conflict that can occur if the secret is discovered is not far from a living hell. Unless you plan to be draconian and chain up your daughter in a dungeon with a chastity belt, or your son on a rack of guilt and despair, you need to prepare yourselves and your teenager for the inevitable time when it will occur. As with the Tax Office, *ignorance is no excuse*. These days no one in a first world country can claim ignorance of the facts of life. The consequences are too great – not only pregnancy for the female, but the potential to contract life threatening diseases for both genders.

Our current education system usually covers most of the bits that lead to sexually transmitted diseases (STDs) and unwanted pregnancy from not using condoms properly, so the theory is known, but that doesn't necessarily lock in the message. If it's not being taught in school, then you need to change schools, or teach it yourself!

As a parent, your own experiences and advice are far more likely to be understood, remembered, and, if you have made some mistakes along the way, avoided. Talking frankly with your teenager in private may help avert a situation that may be life-changing for your entire family. A simple statement requesting your teenager to let you know if he or she is feeling ready for such an event (sexual intercourse) can leave an opening for them to initiate an otherwise awkward conversation at some later time. Hopefully, if your teenager believes he or she can trust you, they will tell you when they feel ready and you can visit your GP and seek his or her advice. Contraceptive options will be explained to you without judgement, and as a fair and open-minded parent living in the 21st century, you also, need to be non-judgemental. If you have strong religious beliefs, then you may need to do some soul-searching. In the end, you will follow your own path and, like all of us, live by the consequences of your own actions.

> I found that an attitude of acceptance of the inevitable helped me cope well over this time and allowed me to maintain a channel of communication and understanding with my teenagers of which I am truly grateful. The love I feel for them is more important than any ego-bruising I might have suffered or pangs of guilt from social conditioning that is based on fear, ignorance or control.

Social behaviour depends upon many things, including the example of the parents. The monogamous and respectful behaviour shown to each other by the parents will tend to be the preferred choice of the children. Every relationship has its ups and downs and sometimes it is difficult to hide the down times from the kids. Your next best option is to minimise the damage done to a young mind and his emotions after seeing and hearing his parent's disagreement. He needs to be told and to understand that it isn't his fault; you still love each other, but sometimes you have differences that need to be sorted out. It would be nice to settle differences reasonably and respectfully all the time, but there will be the odd occasion when the emotions suddenly jump into the fray and take over any peaceful negotiation. This is part of life.

Your teenager will watch your behaviour and because it is a learned act, he will tend to replicate it in his future actions. These are the emotional and behavioural tools you are giving your teenager, so every father needs to show the behaviour he wishes his son to emulate and every mother needs to show the behaviour she wishes her daughter to emulate. Be very careful as the wrong impression may also be implanted and can sometimes take much willpower and self-control on the part of your teenager *not* to repeat the mistakes of the parent. This requires your teenager to have a higher awareness of the consequences of certain actions even than his parents. He or she needs to see a few steps ahead, like in a chess game, and work out what will happen if they follow a particular line. The path of least destruction is usually the preferred choice.

Underage drinking must be avoided

I cannot emphasize this point enough. It is simple and straight-forward. *Do not allow your underage teenagers to drink alcohol.* Do not encourage it, thinking it's funny; or who cares anyway; or everybody is doing it now. No, it isn't funny, it's just plain stupid; you, as a parent, should care because the community does and often has to foot the bill for the clean-up; and no, everybody is *not* doing it.

Underage drinking causes totally *avoidable* problems – including the ones that are life-changing. Everything, from the worst case scenario of death to the more moderate one of (just) damage to brain cells, falls within this portfolio. It's a bit like saying, *I know cyanide is a poison and it will kill me, but I just want to try it in case it doesn't,* and then expecting people to take you seriously when you want help.

Some acts of humankind are just stupid and foolish, and underage drinking is one of them. Do you get the message yet? No excuses!

Give your kids advanced driver training

Your older teenagers will naturally want to have their Driver's Licence, so they need to start learning a year or so before they can legally sit the exam. The driving tips I have picked up from my father's wisdom (who taught me to drive) and my own experience, including the Levels 1 and 2 Advanced Driver Training courses (which I thoroughly recommend for all drivers – both, new and old) are located on the website **www.instructionmanual4kids.com**. It is recommended that you show these to your kids when they begin their driver training program.

During the first two or three years of driving – especially if your teenager is not driving very far or very often – encourage him to minimise all distractions in the vehicle, including music and poorly behaved friends. Loud music will affect his ability to hear other road sounds, such as, his car's engine, any emergency vehicles heading his way, potential accidents due to another vehicle locking its brakes, and so on. Additionally, friends who are behaving badly, such as when drunk or if they're just being silly, can cause some anxiety for the inexperienced driver. This may cause him to drive erratically and hence increase the potential for an accident. Instead, put the noisy friends in a taxi; it's not worth it for your kid's peace of mind and possibly his and his friend's lives.

It's *never* too late

I'm a firm believer in the old adage – *while there's life, there's hope!* If you think you have either created or inherited the teenager from hell, I will remind you that there is usually someone out there in a worse situation than yourself. You are not alone; you have not been the first, and you definitely won't be the last.

If you reflect on the issues you now have, you will probably find that a large proportion of them have stemmed from faulty boundaries. Teenagers will push you to the limits and beyond, and if you have established a habit of giving in to his behaviour, he will consider it a victory and continue overstepping your very vague and foggy boundaries. Eventually, he won't even notice he is being disrespectful to you – it's already a habit.

This behaviour needs to be stopped for your teenager's sake, as well as your own. No employer in his right mind will keep an employee who refuses to listen to him and just does what he likes. If your teenager is starting to look for a job, or if he has already been looking, but is unsuccessful so far, it might be worth him considering that a change in attitude might bring him the success he needs.

Encourage your teenager to become involved in some positively focussed daily activity, such as sport or gym work, reading books or magazines, or finding a casual job and working there as often as he can given any family, study or sporting commitments. Back in the seventies, research on different learning methods was undertaken by Ostrander and Schroeder. They discovered that it took 21 days of continuous practice to make or break a habit, so not only was this good for creating good habits, but also for breaking bad ones. This is great because it gives you a direction to follow if you're feeling overwhelmed or uncertain.

Your teenager has a mind and body that needs diversity and activity. Too much of a sedentary lifestyle, such as playing computer games, or sitting on the couch watching movies and eating fast foods, will potentially restrict him to an unhealthy life with a poor self image. As a parent, these are not desired for your teenager. Another interesting finding by Ostrander and Schroeder was that in experiments with music and plants, those plants listening to classic Baroque (Bach) or Indian music (Ravi Shankar) flourished and grew towards the speakers by up to 60 degrees. The plants listening to Rock music shrivelled and died.[64] So, when your teenager is studying, encourage him to

---

[64]   Ostrander, S. and Schroeder, L. 1979, *Superlearning*, pg 91.

avoid rock music and to listen to the Baroque style of classical music if he wishes to give himself the best chance to learn.

Practice *unconditional* love

Earlier I wrote about how a parent can start to feel unappreciated if they have become the unknowing slave to their teenager. If you are spending most of your out-of-school time driving your kids to soccer practice or dance classes, don't worry. That's pretty usual these days, and most of us have done it. I'm talking more about the treatment you receive and the expectations that are placed on you. If your teenager speaks impolitely to you, or hardly speaks at all, especially when you have asked a question, and yet still expects you to have his dinner ready, then you need to break this bond of sufferance, and as soon as possible.

If this behaviour has been going on for some time, then subtle grievances will be taking hold of you. After a few years of running around after him, the resentment you feel has manifested into a reason why your teenager should love and respect you. He doesn't understand this reasoning for the simple reason that you have done this for years, but without mentioning the unwritten contract between you both that has been written in your blood, sweat, and tears. This is a fundamental issue that rears its head in all long term relationships, and it's called *Conditional Love*. One person performs a duty to another under the guise of love, but in reality, there are strings attached:

If I do this for you, then you will promise to love and respect me for the rest of your life!

This is one of the biggest traps a parent can fall into with their children and especially with their teenagers. They won't have a bar of it. What you might have been able to get away with when your child was a toddler or pre-teen, the older teenager is becoming more perceptive and will back away from anything that smells tainted with conditional love. If you're lucky, he may humour you a little and do what you want because he really does love you, but his resentment will build up over time and the simplest request may be enough to snap the fragile bond.

To change this situation, you need to change your attitude about the whole duty-bound thing, get back your dignity, and decide on the boundaries that are immovable. At what point will you say *No* and really mean it. If you don't determine these, you are not doing yourself any benefit, and you are training your teenager that this type of bullying behaviour is acceptable — it isn't, so be strong! Yes, it is painful and might not feel right (this is just trying to break the bad habit), but hold fast and you will be rewarded (eventually).

When you do something for someone else, do it feeling grateful that you have the ability to perform the task. This changes the whole focus and rather than feeling resentment, you start to feel gratitude. As a kid, I used to think how I'd feel if that person died suddenly, and that I wouldn't be able to do anything for him anymore; how petty would my weak arguments be then? So I would do things feeling grateful he was alive and well, but also that I was alive and well, and perfectly capable of doing the tasks too. This helped to put my mind in a better place and the energy around me changed to a calmer and more peaceful level. This allowed me to do things unconditionally – no strings attached – and it is completely liberating. You must try it!

These days, just telling your teenager to do something, won't necessarily work. You need to learn to be a good and savvy negotiator because delicate egos are at stake, and once they are bruised and battered, it takes some time for them to recover. As always your own behaviour is in the spotlight, so you must remain calm, unemotional, and focussed on the point at hand.

I have found that if you simply state your position without the emotions of anger, guilt, or shame attached, your teenager may at least listen and, hopefully after a period of reflection, begin to appreciate your point of view. He might not agree with it, but hopefully understand it better.

For example, if he has been rude to you (in whatever form it takes), you need to tell him that from your perspective, he has been rude to you, he has hurt your feelings by doing so and made you feel unappreciated and disrespected. Ask him if that was his intention, or was he unaware of the hurt he has done. No matter what his answer is, he needs to apologise to you and give you an undertaking that he will be more aware of the situation in future and to do his best to show you the respect you deserve.

If he refuses to do what you ask, then he needs to understand that there are consequences to all actions – whether good or bad. If he seriously refuses to honour you as his parent and continues to treat you with disrespect, while still expecting you to wash his clothes, tidy his room, change his sheets, and cook his meals, then he needs to be made aware that some privileges will be lost. Maybe he won't care if his room looks like a homeless shelter, or his clothes are dirty and smelly, but he will care if the electricity to his computer is restricted to a couple of hours per day (be prepared to take away modems, or turn off power to that part of the house), or that he must prepare his own meals. Negotiate a swap with him, such as an hour's work from him for an hour's extra power to his computer. Work out something that suits your situation.

If other issues, such as substance abuse, are involved, then you need to get professional help; initially from your family doctor, and then take it from there. The behaviour of teenagers, and especially male ones, can be quite erratic and destructive if they are under the influence of drugs. These drugs include alcohol as well as the illicit ones. We have all heard of the bad, and sometimes horrific, events that can be done by people under the influence – both to other people and to themselves. This is a very scary place and needs to be avoided at all costs. If you notice your teenager behaving strangely, becoming suddenly violent or aggressive for no real reason, or being very quiet and depressed, seek medical help and advice. Some drugs, like marijuana, can have a detrimental effect on certain susceptible males after only one exposure. It can induce schizophrenia in males who are predisposed genetically to it. This is a frightening fact and should not be ignored. Marijuana use can often lead to harder drugs, and once this occurs, the downward slide accelerates. Intervention is necessary for any rehabilitation to be successful, and all access and ingestion of drugs must be stopped completely and forever. All drugs are destructive to the body, therefore they should never be ingested in any way at any time. If anyone thinks differently, they are in a state of delusion and that is dangerous. *Taking drugs is absolute stupidity.* Avoid it at all costs!

No assumptions should be made as to your teenager's level of understanding. If he has not been a part of your family for some time, either through a period of separation, or he has come into the home from somewhere else, he will need to have these things explained to him. The experiences he witnessed and endured while he was away from you may have been quite terrible and completely changed his perspective and balance on life. You need to accept that there are some things you may never know about your teenager, but your motivation when dealing with him must stem from a basis of unconditional love, trust, and respect, otherwise he will feel it and cannot respond in kind, even if he wants to.

Our motivation for doing something has to be from a source of purity. If it isn't, then it is faulty and could become destructive. We won't often see ourselves honestly and might not be able to see ourselves through the eyes of our beloved teenagers, so forgive yourself for your mistakes; forgive your teenager for his mistakes; and drop your attachment to all resentments. It is a burden no one need carry. Love your teenager unconditionally and joyfully. He or she is so worth it.

14

Death or Separation

Tell the truth gently and simply.

Instructions:

1. Read the Introduction.
2. Remember energy cannot be created or destroyed.
3. Be prepared to feel a sense of loss.
4. Coping with great pain.
5. Listen to what your heart says.
6. Separation should be respectful and amicable.

This topic is something most people try to avoid as long as possible, but it must be addressed eventually because it will happen to all of us. If your child has a beloved pet, there will come a day when the old cardboard box will have to come out as the makeshift coffin in which to bury their little buddy. Tell your child the plain truth – gently and sincerely. Keep your explanation as simple as possible and, if your child is older, you may be able to explain more about the situation to them.

Kids may surprise you at how well they can grasp a difficult and painful situation.

A little while ago, an email came to me telling the story of a vet who had the unenviable task of euthanizing a family's dog. The dog was old and had lived a perfectly good and loyal life with a loving family. The question, "Why don't dogs live longer?" came up. No one could think of an answer that could possibly explain this reality.

After a period of thought, the young daughter in the family said, "I know why! Because when we are born, we have to learn to live our lives with loyalty, happiness, and unconditional love. Dogs already know this, so they don't have to stay as long."

Just perfect.

Listen to your kids, even the youngest ones, because they often see things from a totally different perspective and can give comfort and clarity.

Remember energy cannot be created or destroyed

From a purely scientific point of view each of us is made up of a huge complexity of specialised cells. As we investigate further and look closely at each component, we discover that each cell is made up of smaller molecules that are grouped in such a way as to perform so many amazing tasks – all the automatic and unconscious tasks that take place within our bodies every single second, minute, and hour of every day. Each of these molecules is made up of atoms, and as has been discussed earlier, they have a lifespan of between seven (7) to ten (10) years in any one body. So even though we may exist on the planet for 70 or 80 years, we have actually completely turned over the atoms in our bodies about 10 times. This means that we have changed physically many times already. Then, if you break these atoms down further, they become a mix of electrons, protons, neutrons, and other sub-atomic particles. If you break down these particles even further, we end up with pure energy.

The first Law of Thermodynamics recognises that energy cannot be made or destroyed; it is always conserved even though it changes form. Keeping this in mind and knowing that we are effectively focal points of energy, unable to be created or destroyed; this intuitively gives rise to the concept that we are immortal. We might not readily exist in the current form we see today, but the very essence of our atoms – pure and intelligent energy – means that we will continue in some form or other after the bodies we currently perceive as *us* are gone into the dust.

At the point of death, our lost loved one is no longer with us in the form that was familiar to us. The intelligent energy that controls the life force, and hence the systems, within their body has been transformed into an alternative energy form that most of us cannot observe.

Be prepared to feel a sense of loss

When a death occurs in a family, the first thing you notice is the absence of that person. It is permanent and it is incredibly painful – it is terrible and you feel like the void that has suddenly appeared in that part of you that used to be your heart will never close over and heal. Whether it is a cherished pet, a beloved parent, sibling, relative or friend, there is nothing you can do to change it. The reaction of those who are left behind varies considerably and is entirely dependent upon the relationship they shared with the departed one.

A common reaction is *regret* because you start to remember the times when you didn't listen to him, or take him seriously, or spoke harshly to him, or treated him badly. You particularly remember the last time you spoke with him or spent time with him. You go over the dialogue: *what did he say, what did I say?* Any little sarcastic emphasis, or gesture of impatience, or word spoken in haste and anger starts to play around in your mind and becomes larger with each repetition of the scene. Then, dripping in guilt and grief, you ask yourself, *When did I last tell him I loved him?* You mentally beat yourself up and find all the reasons why you are the worst person in the world. There is no penance this way, only mental trauma, emotional anguish, and further despair.

When my son decided to join the army, as a mother, I considered the possible consequences of his action. I could follow one of two potential paths: the first one was that he would be all right and survive the rigours of the training and service; and the second was that he wouldn't. If I chose to focus on the latter, I knew I would be taking a path of misery and pain. So I *chose* to take the former path.

This path is one of joy in seeing my boy doing something he loves and something that is worthwhile for the lifestyle we hold so dear. I never tried to talk him out of it. I just made sure he knew it was what he most wanted at that point in his life.

I cried on the morning of his enlistment and gave him a big hug because I knew this would be his last day as a boy. The next time I would see him, he would be a man – his own man. I could see an army life was a means to an end for him, so my husband and I encouraged him to do his best to learn well and we were able to share in his moments of accomplishment. Every parent, or family member, watching the graduating recruitment platoon was so proud of their child – boy or girl; man or woman.

On his first deployment to Afghanistan, I *chose* to feel his feelings of excitement and adventure, and refused to let my feelings develop into anything sad or fearful. This was his first trip overseas without mum and dad and at the ripe old age of 19, he was bright eyed and bushy-tailed; ready to go. We were there at the airport to see him off and we were happy for him. We shared a quick and meaningful hug, then he steadfastly walked away from us to the Customs area without looking back. I'm inclined to think his feelings of 'it's now or never' might have been threatening to overwhelm him a little as well.

I will be eternally grateful for the quality of telecommunications at this time because it enabled us to keep in contact with him by email, social media, and the telephone. We were unable to contact him directly, but he called us on average about once a week – a far cry from the unreliable and slow mail services during past wars. We also sent him packages of some of his favourite snacks, shows and movies on computer hard drives, magazines, and other bits and pieces. While he was away, I thought only of seeing him at a happy time in the future – perhaps with a couple of kids, or standing in front of his new house.

The first time we saw him again when he returned home was just wonderful. Here he was, actually in front of us in the flesh. He looked like he had grown and his trolley of gear was so laden, we were amazed he could actually carry it all. He saw us and a huge smile transformed his face into a mixture of happiness, slight embarrassment, and relief.

In the days and weeks to follow, we heard many stories that amazed and surprised us. He had learned so much about another culture so very different from our own. And he had learned to cope with extremes of weather, temperature, living conditions, and trauma. His levels of tolerance and patience had grown exponentially. His naturally happy nature was still there, and now it was expressed with a quiet confidence and wisdom drawn from some of life's hardest experiences and that was a delight to see.

Indeed, our boy had come home a man.

While our son was away in Afghanistan, I decided to learn some more about his career path and picked up a couple of books from his shelf. One book recounted the time when a large number of troops were dropped behind enemy lines in an area that was supposed to be clear. It wasn't, and for the next 18 hours, the soldiers were battered with all manner of weaponry. There were 87 men dropped into that zone, and after that horrendous amount of time, incredibly all 87 of them were lifted out – albeit some with massive injuries.

Another story, this time from an acquaintance, recalls an occasion when her daughter was newly engaged and members from both families were enjoying a night out for dinner. While they were all sitting there enjoying the meal and the conversation, her daughter's prospective father-in-law gently dropped his head to one side like he was sleeping. He didn't respond to gentle queries and then they realised he wasn't breathing. Her husband applied CPR for 20 minutes until paramedics arrived but he was pronounced dead as a result of a massive heart attack.

One more story I have is about a friend who died in her early 40's. This lady was a devoted mother, a truly happy and generous person, who loved to help anyone she could if they needed it. She was the type of person who always remembered birthdays and special occasions, and her Christmas baskets were always colourful and cheerful. Every little detail was attended to and no trouble to herself. She lived a healthy and spiritual life and practiced loving kindness and meditation. Then, one day she was attending to her garden in her backyard and her heart just stopped beating. There was no logical reason why something like that should happen to such a wonderful person – it just did.

I mention these stories because they confirm for me something that many people say, but not many really believe: *when our time is up, it's up and when it's not, it's not.* No matter where you are or what you're doing (or not doing), when it's your time to depart this life, then you'll just go and there is nothing anyone can do to prevent it. That is the illusion and the cause of many people to feel a sense of guilt when someone dies tragically or suddenly. No parent should blame himself for *causing* his child to die, especially if he has given the child a toy or a gift that has been the means by which the child's life has been taken away. There can be no guilt regarding when the death occurs because I don't believe there is any impact that anyone can have on the *timing* of another's death. In other words, if the child was not meant to die, then he would have lived.

A family from our kid's local school tragically lost one of their sons in a trail bike accident a short time after he received the bike as a gift from his parents. The school community came together to support the family during this horrible time of grief and the kids were very respectful and empathetic to the remaining family members.

I do not want to imagine what these parents were feeling at the time, but I hope for their sake, that they were not riddled with *guilt* for giving their son a gift that he was absolutely thrilled about and excited to ride.

This does not give you an excuse to be an irresponsible parent. You must still provide as safe a place as possible for your child. Injuries are still a threat to a child and to their quality of life. A person might still feel guilt based on their *treatment* of the person or their lack of responsibility and care while they were alive. That is still a very real and concerning issue. So be vigilant and aware of potential hazards and minimise the risks around the home. That is within your sphere of control. Just know that accidents do happen and no matter what effort a parent puts in to prevent them, they can still occur.

Also, people can be put into a situation whereby they have the means to take another's life, such as being a soldier. But the reality of whether a person dies is up to his life's journey coming to its close.

Coping with great pain

When you lose or separate from a cherished loved one, your emotions are extremely volatile. There are varying depths of despair from which you might feel that you can never recover. Then you may have a fleeting lighter moment, only to plunge back into darkness and fear again. You shut yourself off from the outside world vowing it can never be the same as it once was. And it won't. It doesn't always end up as a bad thing, but it always feels bad at the start. Depending upon your special connection with your departed loved one, the effect on you and the time to recover will differ.

If you were a close family and you lived in the same house, it may take you a very long time to accept the situation – many years for some people. The hollowness you feel deep inside you; the grief and panic that sits somewhere in your throat, threatens to rise up and engulf you at the mere sniff of a beloved scent. His room, his place at the dinner table, his clothes and possessions are all constant reminders of his presence. There are memories of him in every corner and shadow of your life.

If you were distant family, friends, workmates or schoolmates, you should be able to recover in a shorter time frame because there will be places in your life which you didn't share with him, so the memories will be restricted to specific places and will lessen over time.

If you are younger, you may feel like you have lost a trusted mentor who once inspired and encouraged you to go on to great things. Or he may have showed you a level of respect that made you feel so special – no one else could see your potential the way he did. Fear may become the dominant emotion at this time in your life because the stability has been shattered for some time.

If you are older, you may feel anger or frustration at the waste of a youthful life gone forever. This may force you to consider your own life choices and possibly leave you feeling like so much of your own life has been wasted. You then have two choices to make: continue down the same pathway, or at some future point, be inspired to change direction and achieve something great for yourself.

The textbooks tell us there are five stages of grief:

1. Denial – *No, I don't believe it, I won't believe it!*
2. Anger – *This is rubbish! It's not fair! WHY did it happen to him?*
3. Bargaining – *Please, please take me instead. I'll do anything!*
4. Depression – *It's too late. I'll never be happy again.*
5. Acceptance – *He's gone. I can't change it. I need to move on.*

When grief happens to us, we pass through each of these stages; a little faster through some than others, but for us to be able to continue to live fulfilling and happy lives, we need to pass through them all until acceptance releases us from the burden of attachment.

Acceptance and release doesn't mean you will forget that person or pet. Your memories will stay with you throughout your lifetime; you should cherish all the happy ones, and learn from the sad ones. Do not dwell on the sad memories however, because that will put you in a place where there is no joy and that is to be avoided. If you stay there, you are likely to become bitter about life in general, and other people will not find any pleasure in your company. Empathy and patience wears off after some time and friends will be lost.

When I was about 11 years old, my cousin from Thailand came to stay with us and he went to a local grammar school. He became a close part of our family from that time and even after he went to a well-respected boarding school, that was over 100 km away, he maintained ties with us by coming home during the mid-year school holidays, and dropping back on the weekends when our favourite footy team was playing at its home ground near where we lived.

I loved those times because he had become a fine young man; willing to help with the dishes *and* putting up with his little cousin who adored and appreciated him like a special brother. He often brought his friends from school who were all great young men – full of life; loving to joke around and share happy times. They even took me to the footy sometimes when the match was being played at another club's ground. I loved the footy, and I loved them all, especially for taking the time to think of me and of what I wanted, and not to push me away as a pesky cousin.

I remember asking him one evening (while he was drying the dishes) what he thought of me. As a 14 year old, it felt important for me to have an image of myself reflected in the eyes of someone who I respected so much. He thought for a while and then simply said, "I love you." Maybe he was being very diplomatic because he saw my obvious lack of self-confidence and other insecurities attributed to most young teenagers. But, whatever the reason, it was an answer that I could accept with gratitude, even though I may not have appreciated its full meaning at the time.

A few short months later, my mother answered the phone at 7:30 one morning. She cried out, took in a gasp of air, and then was silent. She turned to us and halting said that Charlie had died. Then, she had the horrific task of calling her sister in Thailand to break the dreadful news to her. My 18 year old cousin had been found slumped on the grass that morning after he had apparently been jogging around one of the ovals. According to the coroner's report, he died as a result of an infection in his heart.

My life had just become a blur of confusion, deep lows, fractional highs, and uncontrollable sadness.

The only person I knew (with the possible exception of my father) who seemed to understand and appreciate me was gone, and gone forever. This was my frightening, gut-wrenching reality at the time, and I went through all the stages of grief – particularly the bargaining part, but it didn't work, no matter what I offered. I talked to him often, both in my mind and sometimes out loud when no one was around. I questioned motives, but got no satisfactory answers. Why? – was a common question burnt into my brain. I cried until the tears threatened to dry up, and then strangely, sometimes I laughed, when only moments before I was struck with the deepest sadness. The emotional roller-coaster was the pits, but through it all, I had one rock to hold onto – I knew my cousin loved me.

My life had changed forever; I withdrew into my own thoughts and feelings, and became more detached from people in general. Meditation and reflection helped a lot, probably more than I knew, and it was a little over a year later when the love of my life briefly appeared on my horizons, and blossomed into a life-long relationship a couple of years later.

Once again, my life changed forever, but this time in a very joyful and positive direction. The sun shone and the stars came out again.

Listen to what your heart says

Every religion or belief system has its own, sometimes unique, perspective on death; a discussion of which is well beyond the scope of this book. Neither is it my intention to comment further than to say it is entirely up to the individual as to whether they wish to follow any particular religious belief. Remember that religions are born from the human perspective or interpretation of the life and behaviour of a very special person. Most of these people did not desire to be made into a *religion*, but to merely have their actions and behaviour followed and repeated for the betterment of all humans. Unfortunately, I believe too much human interference in the ensuing years has distorted the original intentions of these great avatars, so use your discretion and listen to what your heart tells you before you choose any path to follow.

Separation should be respectful and amicable

Grief over separation can be just as painful as a death, but it usually doesn't last as long because the person is still alive. Other emotions, such as anger and resentment, are often felt very strongly and the length of some of the grief stages may vary considerably, even for many years especially if the separation is not complete, so resentment and bitterness can develop further with the passing of the years.

It is a sad and sobering fact that many marriages end in divorce (about 50% in the US and over 30% in Australia[65]). Of those relationship breakups, nearly half of them involve children.[66] This means that about one out of every two or three of us are pretty hopeless when it comes to creating and nurturing a wholesome relationship. Now, if you're standing there pointing at your spouse, don't blame him or her for the hell you're in. Take your share of the responsibility, whether you're a victim or a tyrant. Each of us attracts into our lives what we need to learn in this lifetime, so forget the blame game, recognise your part in the basic failure – a lack of tolerance or a lack of self-worth – and change your life for the better.

---

[65] http://www.abs.gov.au/AUSSTATS/abs@.nsf/Lookup/4102.0Main+Features40Sep+2010

[66] http://www.abs.gov.au/ausstats/abs@.nsf/Products/413113F61FD056ADCA2577ED00146265?opendocument

When you realise that life has become intolerable with your partner and there are no more fixes to try, friends with whom to discuss things, or counsellors with whom to consult, a separation is inevitable. Accept this and be as respectful of each other as you can be, as you carve up the family possessions. The pain becomes acute when children are involved because they need to have a continuing relationship with both parents. Unless one of the parents is unstable in a real way, any separation must have shared responsibility with both the male and the female parent. Too many issues have stemmed from a lack of involvement, especially by the father, because they are least likely to gain full custody, or even an equal share of a joint custody decision.

When you look at a separation from a child's point of view, you will see that they may have very different feelings about the situation compared with their parents. Often they will feel that they are to blame for the separation; they are confused about what has happened; and they only want their parents to be reconciled. They may not have seriously considered the arguments, bickering, and the unkindness that was occurring between the parents, sometimes for many years. If they were physically involved, they may have learned to avoid the worst times and run away from the build up to explosive moments.

In many cases, despite the obvious unhappiness between the parents, the child still wants their parents' love and companionship to be renewed. Sometimes this is possible, but only by the concerted effort of both parents wanting a similar outcome. Each parent has to recognise their own part in the breakdown of the relationship, and they have to be willing to change their behaviour and thinking for any renewal to have a chance of lasting longer than a few months.

After 19 years of marriage, my husband, Frank, and I had our first separation. We had not been communicating well for some time – a few years if I am really honest – and even though we tried to support each other, something was wrong and it just wasn't happening.

Frank said that we needed to separate and that we would share in the care of the kids one week on and one week off. I could move in to my parent's nearby holiday unit, and he would find another one to rent during the weeks he was off duty. Obviously, he had thought about this for some time and had planned the whole thing to try and be amicable – from his perspective.

For myself, on the other hand, I tried unsuccessfully to see his point of view and what he was attempting, but I was so far in the dark, I didn't really understand why we were separating in the first place! Why was it necessary?

Well, in reality, it never really came about because we were quite bad at separating. Frank had found a place to rent and moved in there, but he spent most of his time back with us because I became very sick – I developed epilepsy. I used to have a seizure in the pre-waking stages of sleep, so (apart from one occasion) they always occurred when I was in bed and quite infrequently – months apart. So, even though we had gone through the pain of the *thought* of separation – and put the kids through it – it wasn't that much different from what it was before.

We did start a period of counselling and that helped me to understand my issues and especially my lack of self-esteem and propensity to behave like a victim. I didn't always feel like a victim, but I did around my husband. The strange thing was that he felt the same – he felt like I was bullying him! Self-delusion and lack of clarity can do strange things to one's mind and we were both guilty of it.

After a few months, we tried our marriage again, but we hadn't gone too far down the track when things were obviously not right, so we separated briefly for a second time. We sold our house and rented another one while this turmoil was going on and made some really bad financial decisions. Even though we were both working (me from home, Frank from an office), we didn't seem to be able to save any money – having four kids might have had something to do with this, but our collective mindset was not framed around thoughts of abundance, but more the opposite – thoughts of lack.

Finally, after bouncing up and down on the emotional roller-coaster again and again, I realised that things may have changed a little, but the underlying issues were still there. The trust and respect were missing in large chunks – they were there sometimes and in some circumstances, but they were not there all the time for every occasion. I had now come to understand that a separation was inevitable, and that this time it had to be done properly – little or no personal contact for about three months. This last time, I had accepted the fact that he still didn't have any emotional trust in me, and I was tired of telling him otherwise. He had to go and live somewhere else, while I wanted some peace and time to think about what I wanted from my life.

The kids were aged between 11 and 17, and by this time, they had come to accept our separations as just another drama in life, and not really anything to be too concerned about – after all, life didn't really change. They still saw their father almost as much as before, and when they did see him, he was more attentive and respectful of their needs and wishes than he was prior to all this happening. At the time of our first separation, they were all in their pre-teen years, and the thought of not having their parents together was absolutely traumatic. The effect on them by this first separation was far greater than any subsequent one.

Eventually, after many months of self-analysis, meditation, visualisation, and forgiveness, we were able to renew our vows to each other in front of our children and continue with our marriage from a more balanced and unconditionally loving platform. We recently celebrated 33 years of marriage.

I have also been seizure-free for over five years.

Become the best person you can be

To recover and move on from feelings of guilt or ineptitude, you need to start believing in yourself again. One way to start this process is to change the way you speak to and treat people now. Pick yourself up as well as you can with the awareness that there will still be periods of depression and sadness. Get yourself out of the doldrums and remind yourself of the lesson you have to learn here – tell all your family, and those you really care about, that you love them. Do this every time they are leaving for work or school in the morning, or going back to their own home after visiting you. Finish your telephone conversations with *I love you* and really be sincere about it. Treat those you love as if you might not have the opportunity to speak with them again.

Do not take anyone you care about for granted.

Increase your level of tolerance with those around you and avoid petty arguments; they achieve nothing. Really try to be the person you wish you were. So think of the great aspects that this *best of you* would have; what are the types of things you would say; what would you do for others you love; how can you change yourself to be that best person you know you can be.

When you have thought about these answers, write them down in a journal or somewhere special where they won't be lost or thrown away. Then you can read them any time you like – in the beginning at least twice a day; morning and night.

After a time, the repetition of these kind and positive messages will pass from your conscious mind to your subconscious mind and they will happen without your forced intervention.

Then, you will have become the best person you can be and that is the greatest achievement.

15

Final Words

Be a tourist, not a local!

What's the difference between a *tourist* and a *local*?

A tourist is usually on holidays, so he spends his time looking at all the sights around him. He *observes* many things, like the trees and birds, the people and their culture, and the natural and man-made wonders. The attitude he has when he observes is generally a mixture of wonder, enthusiasm, and joy. He delights in everything new, takes plenty of happy snaps and walks a lot so he can take his time to see the places more closely. His focus is on what's right with this world. He doesn't claim it as his own.

Now, what does a local do? He is either driving around in circles trying to get things done (and not necessarily achieving much) or he is sitting around griping about things, including all the tourists around the place. The local is usually so caught up in his daily activity (rut) that he doesn't see the birds or blue sky, or revel in the amazing colours of a perfect sunset, or delight in the perfume of a fragrant flower. He may often make harsh *judgements* about others and complain about his lot in life. He tends to see the rubbish in the gutters, the weeds in the gardens, and the smog in the air. His focus is on what's wrong with his world and he is firmly attached to it.

In each case, the environment is the same, but the *attitude* and subsequent behaviour towards the life around each one is completely different – this is the individual's choice.

If you *observe*, rather than *judge*, then you see simple facts, unbridled by emotions. It puts you on the same level as everyone around you. When we make a judgement, we are artificially placing ourselves in a superior position to those about whom we judge. What right have we to do that? Absolutely, none! Energetically, we are all equal. At an atomic level, we are so similar, we wouldn't know the difference. The structure of each being and every object on the planet is 99.999% empty space and 0.001% pure intelligent energy.

We are just *focal points* of that intelligent energy. Everything else that we perceive as real is just a distraction.

I like to think that we are all pieces on a big cosmic board game, and the universe is tossing the dice and moving the pieces around the board. Every opportunity is like picking up a *Here's an Opportunity* card. And every challenge is a *Take a Chance* card. Every so often we land on the *Tax Owing* square, or the *Congratulations! You have a New Baby* square. Sometimes, we land on the *In the Poop* square, and this might be a choice of divorce, separation, death or prison. The dice keeps rolling on and on, and we, the pieces, keep getting moved around and around. After a while, you stop becoming attached to things and you realise it's just another roll of the dice. Things come and things go.

So, release your attachments to the things around you, including the behaviours some of us so desperately cling to when we are under stress or emotionally challenged in some way. Let go of the desire to *worry* about things that have happened, are happening, or what might happen. We have no control over any of this; we can only do the best we can now, in this present moment.

Spend some quiet time reflecting on how your own mental and physical improvement will put you in a happier place, and how this will flow down to benefit your children and instil this positive attitude in them.

Your kids make your life complete. They can be challenging, frustrating, annoying, and disappointing, but they can also be inspiring and amusing, and will extract feelings of such pride, gratitude, and love from your very depths, that you cannot imagine from where they have sprung. Just let it happen.

Treasure each moment you have with your wonderful kids. They do grow up very quickly and one day will leave home and make their own way in life. Hopefully, they will want you to share their journey with them and continue to be a loving parent, friend, and mentor.

This is what I hope for you.

About the Author

Kerri Yarsley was born in Melbourne, Australia back in the late 1950's and grew up among an evolving multicultural society – her own mother being Thai born to Australian-Thai parents. The diverse mix of Anglo-Asian and Mediterranean cultures in which she grew up helped to mould her views of fairness and equality for all.

Her childhood was not wracked by emotionally disturbed relatives, but was instead quite normal and generally happy. She had the same dreams and self-confidence issues as most girls, but always had a feeling that life would be good.

After Kerri's beloved cousin died at 18 years of age, she became a little more serious and it changed her perspective on life. A year later, she met her lifetime sweetheart, Frank. She went to university for five years of full-time study and attained qualifications in Biochemistry and Microbiology (BSc), Education (Dip Ed) and Computers (Grad Dip Comp Sc) – a surprising mix of subjects, but exactly the ones that have enabled her to be where she is now. She worked as a Computer Systems Programmer for several years, while maintaining a high level of health and fitness with Frank – both attaining Fitness Leader's qualifications, and being involved with martial arts training, prior to starting their family.

Kerri and Frank wanted four children close together – boy, girl, boy, girl – and that is exactly what they got, roughly two years apart. Imagine living with four children under six years of age! As their young family grew, Kerri began contract documenting from home and this allowed her to keep up with current technological and business trends. She has been a Technical Writer now for nearly 20 years and recently qualified with a Diploma in Business.

With each other's support, and the help of the odd nanny or three, childcare centres, kindergartens, schools, and external cultural, sporting or martial arts schools, Kerri and Frank have pursued their various goals and ambitions; maintaining their underlying philosophy of continuing education throughout life. They continue to enjoy sharing good times and spirited communications with their four incredibly different and wonderful kids – now 27, 25, 23 and 21 years of age.

The author, her husband, and their four children taken in 2009.

Bibliography

The following books and references have been sources of inspiration, understanding, and information for this book and my life:

Astrand, P.-O. and Rodahl, K. 1977, *Textbook of Work Physiology: Physiological Bases of Exercise*, 2nd edn, McGraw-Hill Inc, New York, USA.

Bays, Brandon. 1999, *The Journey: An extraordinary guide for healing your life and setting yourself free*, Thorsons, an imprint of Harper-Collins Publishers, Hammersmith, UK.

Benyus, J. M. 1997, *Biomimicry: Innovation Inspired by Nature*, Harper Perennial, HarperCollins Publishers Inc, New York, USA.

Ajahn Brahm. 2004, *Opening the Door of Your Heart: And other Buddhist Tales of Happiness*, Thomas C. Lothian Pty Ltd, South Melbourne, Australia.

Chopra, Deepak. 1989, *Quantum Healing: Exploring the Frontiers of Mind/Body Medicine*, Bantam Books, New York, USA.

Chopra, Deepak. 2006, *Power, Freedom, and Grace: Loving from the Source of Lasting Happiness*, Amber-Allen Publishing Inc, San Rafael, USA.

Clason, George S. 1955, *The Richest Man in Babylon*, E. P. Dutton, Signet Books, and New American Library, divisions of Penguin Books USA Inc, New York, USA.

HH Dalai Lama & Cutler, H.C. 1999, *The Art of Happiness: A Handbook for Living*, Hodder Headline Australia Pty Ltd, Sydney, Australia.

Daly, S. & Hartmann, P. *Infant Demand and Milk Supply – Part 1 Infant Demand and Milk Production in Lactating Women*. Journal of Human Lactation I, 1995; **1**: 21-26.

Daly, S.E., Di Rosso, A., Owens, R.A. & Hartmann, P.E. *Degree of Breast Emptying Explains Changes in the Fat Content, but Not Fatty Acid Composition, of Human Milk*. Experimental Physiology, 1993; **78**: 741-755.

Deardorff, J., et al. *Father Absence, Body Mass Index, and Pubertal Timing in Girls: Differential Effects by Family Income and Ethnicity*. Journal of Adolescent Health, 2011 May, **48**(5): 441-447.

de Bono, E. 1992, *Teach Your Child How To Think*, Penguin Books Ltd, Harmondsworth, UK.

Doidge, N. 2008, *The Brain That Changes Itself*, Viking/Penguin Group Inc, New York, USA.

Dyer, Wayne W. 1989, *You'll See It When You Believe It*, Schwartz Publishing, Melbourne, Australia.

Ekman, P. 2009, *Telling Lies*, W.W. Norton & Company Inc, New York, USA.

Fowler, H.W. & Fowler, F.G. (eds) 1970, *The Concise Oxford Dictionary*, 5th edn, Oxford University Press, London, UK.

Fries, J.F., Vickery, D.M., Telford, R.D. & Reid R.A. 2001, *Take Care of Yourself*, Australian Edition, Addison-Wesley Publishers Ltd, Boston, USA.

Frisén, J., Spalding, K.L., Bhardwaj, R.D., Buchholz, B.A. & Druid, H. *Retrospective Birth Dating of Cells in Humans*. Cell Journal, 2005 July; **122**: 133-43.

Goldman, AS. *The immune system of human milk antimicrobial, antiinflammatory and immunomodulating properties*. Pediatrics Infectious Disease Journal, 1993 Aug; **12**(8): 664-71.

Gray, John. 1992, *Men are from Mars, Women are from Venus*, Thorsons, an imprint of HarperCollins Publishers, Hammersmith, UK.

Hawkins, David R. 1998, *Power versus Force: An Anatomy of Consciousness – The Hidden Determinants of Human Behaviour*, Veritas Publishing, Sedona, USA.

Hay, L.L. 1988, *Heal Your Body*, 4th edn, Specialist Publications, Concord, Australia.

Hay, L.L. 1999, *You Can Heal Your Life*, Hay House Australia Pty Ltd, Brighton-Le-Sands, Australia.

Hill, N. 1979, *Law of Success*, 4th edn, Success Unlimited, Division of W. Clement Stone PMA Communications Inc, Illinois, USA.

Jensen, Bernard. 2000, *Dr. Jensen's Guide to Diet and Detoxification*, Keats Publishing, Division of NTC/Contemporary Publishing Group Inc, Illinois, USA.

Kelleher, S.L. and Lonnerdal, B. *Immunological Activities Associated with Milk*. Advances in Nutritional Research, 2001; **10**: 39-65.

Lehninger, Albert L. 1975, *Biochemistry*, 2nd edn, Worth Publishers Inc, New York, USA.

Moore, Pete. 2002, *E=mc² The great ideas that shaped our world*, New Burlington Books, Quintet Publishing Limited, London, UK.

Ostrander, S. & Schroeder, L. with Ostrander, N. 1981, *Superlearning*, Sphere Books Ltd, London, UK.

Peterson, L. & Renstrom, P. 1986, *Sports Injuries: Their Prevention and Treatment*, Methuen Australia, North Ryde, Australia.

Swami Ramakrishnananda Puri. 2003, *Racing Along the Razor's Edge: Discourses on Spirituality*, Mata Amritanandamayi Center, San Ramon, USA.

Rikard-Bell, R. 1990, *Loving Sex: Happiness in* Mateship, Wypikaninkie Publications, Brighton-Le-Sands, Australia.

Ross, J.S. & Wilson, K.J.W. 1981, *Foundations of Anatomy and Physiology* 5th edn, Churchill Livingstone, Edinburgh, UK.

Rowe, D. 2010, *Why We Lie: The Source of Our Disasters*, Harper Collins, Australia.

Salans, L.B., Cushman, S.W. & Weismann, R.E., *Studies of Human Adipose Tissue Adipose Cell Size and Number in Nonobese and Obese Patients.* Journal of Clinical Investigation, 1973 April; **52**(4): 929–41.

Schlosser, Eric. 2002, *Fast Food Nation.* Penguin Books Ltd, London, UK.

Shetty, P. 2010, *Nutrition, Immunity & Infection.* Commonwealth Agricultural Bureaux International (CABI), Wallingford, UK.

Spalding, K.L., et al. *Dynamics of fat cell turnover in humans.* Nature Journal, 2008 June; **453**: 783-87.

Statham, Bill. 2011, *The Chemical Maze Shopping Companion*, 10th Anniversary edn, POSSIBILITY.COM, Loch, Australia.

Thomson, W.A.R. 1973, *Thomson's Concise Medical Dictionary*, Churchill Livingstone, Edinburgh, UK.

Tracey, D.J., Baume, P., et al. 2000, *Anatomica*, Random House Australia Pty Ltd, Milsons Point, Australia.

Waitley, Denis E. 1979, *The Psychology of Winning: Ten Qualities of a Total Winner*, Winners.Inter.National, Adelaide, Australia.

White, Dorothy. 1995, *Reiki: The Energy of Life in the Spirit of Love*, Dorothy White, Brisbane, Australia.

Xanthou, M. *Immune protection of human milk.* Biology of the Neonate. 1998 Aug; **74**(2):121-33.

Websites and Other Resources for Parents

Australian Broadcasting Corporation:
www.abc.net.au/health/thepulse/stories/2006/08/10/1710593.htm

Answers.com – Wiki and Reference Answers:
www.answers.com/topic/composition-of-the-body

Australian Breastfeeding Association:
http://www.breastfeeding.asn.au/

Australian Bureau of Statistics:
www.abs.gov.au/AUSSTATS/abs@.nsf/mf/3101.0

Beyond Blue – Postnatal Depression:
    http://www.beyondblue.org.au/index.aspx?link_id=94
Car seat and capsule fitters (Australia):
    http://www.crep.com.au/authorised-restraint-fitting-stations.html
Circle of Moms – Motherhood, Shared and Simplified – USA:
    http://www.circleofmoms.com/
The Chemical Maze:
    www.chemicalmaze.com
13Health – Queensland Government Health, confidential advice service:
    http://www.health.qld.gov.au/13health/
Journal of Adolescent Health:
    http://jahonline.org/article/S1054-139X(10)00389-7/abstract
Lifeline – Crisis support service:
    http://www.lifeline.org.au/
Molecular Medicine Today:
    http://www.biominerais.com.br/artigos/alumiantipe.pdf
Only the Breast – Breast milk services in the USA and UK:
    http://www.onlythebreast.com
    http://www.onlythebreast.co.uk
Poisons Information Australia:
    http://lifeinthefastlane.com/2008/11/poisons-information-australia/
American Association of Poison Control Centers:
    http://www.aapcc.org/DNN/
SIDS and Kids – safe sleeping website:
    http://www.sidsandkids.org/safe-sleeping/
About.com – Sports Medicine:
    http://sportsmedicine.about.com/od/fitnessevalandassessment/a/
    Body_Fat_Comp.htm
The New York Times:
    http://www.nytimes.com/2009/08/11/health/research/11cancer.html
Tresillian Family Care Centre – Australian child and family health
    organisation:
    http://www.tresillian.net/
    http://www.tresillian.net/tresillian-tips/settling-techniques-newborn-
    12-months.html
Wikipedia:
    http://en.wikipedia.org/wiki/Vitamin_D